contents

introduction

Portmeirion

As I travel through beautiful landscapes in Europe I'm often struck by the lack of aesthetics or charm in the recently built housing. As I drove through the stunning tapestry-like hills of North Wales, imagine my delight when I arrived at the village of Portmeirion.

First off, one feels one is entering a fantasy hill town in Italy. Wondrous shapes and domes, steeples and a variety of different roof lines all in an extraordinary palette of high pastels, cobalt blues and rusty golds. Built around a basin, these delightfully shaped buildings and pergolas are arranged at different heights with winding paths and cobbled stairs to help visitors explore – like children on a 'jungle gym'.

LEFT, BELOW AND OPPOSITE: Scenes from Portmeirion. Clough William-Ellis, a Welsh architect, lovingly built Portmeirion from 1926 to 1976 to demonstrate that a beautiful site could be developed in a sensitive, imaginative way.

Kaffe Fassett's
QUILT ROMANCE

featuring Roberta Horton • Mary Mashuta • Liza Prior Lucy • Pauline Smith
• Brandon Mably • Sally Davis • Pam Goecke Dinndorf • Kim McLean

A ROWAN PUBLICATION

The Taunton Press

The Taunton Press
Inspiration for hands-on living®

The Taunton Press, Inc., 63 South Main Street, PO Box 5506, Newtown, CT 06470-5506
email: tp@taunton.com

First published in Great Britain in 2009 by
Rowan Yarns
Green Lane Mill
Holmfirth
West Yorkshire
England
HD9 2DX

Art Director:	Kaffe Fassett
Technical editors:	Ruth Eglinton and Pauline Smith
Co-ordinator:	Pauline Smith
Publishing Consultant:	Susan Berry
Patchwork Designs:	Kaffe Fassett, Roberta Horton, Mary Mashuta, Liza Prior Lucy, Pauline Smith, Brandon Mably, Sally Davis, Pam Goecke Dinndorf, Kim McLean
Feature:	Kim McLean
Quilters:	Judy Irish, Pauline Smith
Sewers for Liza Prior Lucy quilts:	Judy Baldwin, Corienne Kramer
Photography:	Debbie Patterson
Flat shot photography:	Dave Tolson @ Visage
Styling:	Kaffe Fassett
Design Layout:	Christine Wood - Gallery of Quilts cover/front section Simon Wagstaff - instructions & technical information
Illustrations:	Ruth Eglinton

Library of Congress Cataloging-in-Publication Data

Fassett, Kaffe.
  Kaffe Fassett's quilt romance / featuring Roberta Horton ... [et al.].
    p. cm. -- (Patchwork and quilting book number ; 11)
  ISBN 978-1-60085-259-6
  1. Patchwork--Patterns. 2. Quilting--Patterns. I. Title. II. Title: Quilt
romance.
  TT835.F3676 2009
  746.46'041--dc22
                              2009016377

Colour reproduction by Chroma Graphics (Overseas) Pte. Ltd
Printed and bound in Singapore by KHL. Printing Co. Pte. Ltd

What a setting for our quilts. In a small space we had every possible background for the moods of our quilts; for a pale one the pastel tones of this row of cottages, for a deeper palette the rich husky tones of a terracotta building with singing turquoise details. Statues, carved architraves and clever plaster work made even quite ordinary shaped buildings have a jaunty elegance and work as an ensemble.

As soon as we knew we would use this great location all of us quilt makers began to make quilts that would sing on these multi-coloured walls. Noticing how benches and many architectural details were painted a high turquoise, I used that colour in several quilts and did my *Ice Cream* quilt in milky blue and white to go with the cobalt and chalky white of the alcove below the village hotel.

Not content to build a magical village Clough also devised an enchanting garden complete with Chinese pagodas for inhabitants to wander through. These made delicious settings for our various quilts.

As you peruse this book I think you will agree with me that a little loving attention and lots of drive can produce aesthetically pleasing housing for our needy planet.

OPPOSITE TOP: Kaffe's *Hearts And Gizzards* on the fresh blue and white of the lower terrace

OPPOSITE BELOW: The heart of Portmeirion with its Mediterranean colours.

RIGHT: The delicious high colouring of the ironwork and the many fanciful carvings that lend Portmeirion enchantment.

the fabrics

Asian Circles (left)

Japanese stylized flowers have always been an inspiration to me. It was exciting to create this fabric, bringing together many shapes of flowers I'd seen in old kimonos and oriental embroideries. In Mary Mashuta's *Say It With Flowers And Stripes* it's delightful how the round florals contrast with the lozenges of stripes to very graphic effect.

Millefiore (right)

Paperweights, particularly old Venetian ones have a childlike magic for me. These circles of repeated flower shapes create an intrigue that is hard to stop studying. This fabric is a good addition to the collection of dotty spotties that are so much fun to group together in quilts. I particularly love the way it presents itself as a border in Pauline's *Autumn Daze*.

Big Blooms (left)

Loving polka dot fabrics I thought I would create an upscale dot using round flower forms. It makes a good fabric to use in appliqué or fussy cut. Liza fussy cut the blooms for the centres of her log cabin blocks in *Autumn Log Cabin*.

Lake Blossoms (right)

What is it about the lotus leaf that draws me to it over and over again. I've used it on pottery, in paintings and most successfully in my patchwork fabric collections. The big round shape with bicycle wheel like spokes is so elegant a shape. When you add the pointed graceful blooms it really makes a lush fabric. Its large scale makes this a strong feature in any quilt.

Cabbage Patch (left)

Cabbages to me are like huge roses, so combining them comes naturally to me. I love the way this voluptuous form takes colour combinations so well. It's great to see how people use this print in my different workshops around the world.

Clouds (right)

The oriental world is so studded with brilliant inspirations that many of my designs have their roots there. I have spotted these clouds on Tibetan and Chinese robes for years and had a hunch they would serve the patchworker well, and so they have. The graceful shapes are quite graphic against their plain grounds and have such different effects. Brandon's *Two Up Two Down* uses the high pastel colorway for the sashing and the darker tones are seen in my *Red Flower Power*.

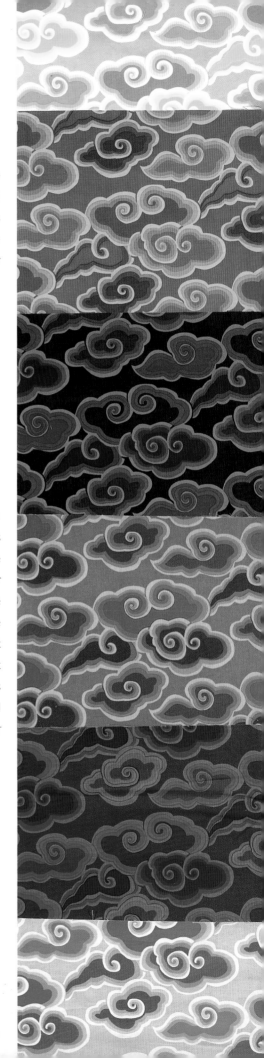

Tall Hollyhocks (below)

When I first got to England hollyhocks seemed to me quintessentially English. I was delighted Philip Jacobs dug up this gorgeous document of a trumpet-like flower. The silvery grey - pink colourway is perfect as the background block in my *Pastel Italian Tiles Quilt*.

Flower Dot (above)

I was given a little book of peasant fabrics from Japan and something similar to this was in that book. The fresh primitive daisy appealed to me and I love the way it appears in my favourite quilt *Pickle Dish*. It's a sort of polka dot with petals.

Lilac Rose (above)

Philip Jacobs has outdone himself with this opulent beauty. I find myself reaching for it over and over when doing big floral quilts. The scale is dramatic enough to really show those overblown roses and lacy lilacs in all the different moods from delicate pastels to passionate reds. In my *Ice Cream* it even works as a narrow ribbon in the softest neutral tones.

11

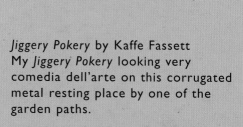

Jiggery Pokery by Kaffe Fassett
My *Jiggery Pokery* looking very
comedia dell'arte on this corrugated
metal resting place by one of the
garden paths.

Hearts and Flowers by Kim McLean
What a valentine this *Hearts and Flowers* quilt
is by Kim. Details show Kim's ingenious use of
my fabrics.

Pastel Italian Tiles by Kaffe Fassett
After my first viewing of the gardens at Portmeirion
I wanted to use the high turquoise of this lattice
work to make my *Pastel Italian Tiles* and that
colouring sure comes to life in this setting.

Ice Cream by Kaffe Fassett
Knowing there was a lot of
Mediterranean white at
Portmeirion I created this
quilt in pale pastel on white
and called it *Ice Cream*.

Cutting Corners by Kaffe Fassett
This quilt is for me the most successful
idea I have come up with to use my
Woven Stripes. The entire quilt uses only
five fabrics, a record for me!

Pickle Dish by Kaffe Fassett
A vintage idea I've been waiting to give my colour treatment to for years. Pauline worked out the pattern and we were off – the colours are perfect for this gloriously toned village.

Say It With Flowers And Stripes by Mary Mashuta
This is another stunning vintage idea that Mary
found and coloured so wonderfully using my
Asian Circles and Multi-stripes. The rich earthy
palette is set off against the terracotta walls of
the Town Hall.

Arrow Feathers by Pam Goecke Dinndorf
Pam's *Arrow Feathers* quilt has the rich resonance of marquetry. Its angles contrast excitingly with the feminine curves of the architecture.

Spring Log Cabin by Liza Prior Lucy
Liza's *Spring Log Cabin* becomes a shimmering
theatre curtain in this garden temple, the soft
pinks echoing the lush hydrangeas.

Magic Carpet by
Roberta Horton
The powerful contrasts
of *Magic Carpet* by
Roberta become a
theatrical happening
when paired with this
grand doorway.

Autumn Log Cabin by
Liza Prior Lucy
Dynamic contrasts gives
power to this quilt by Liza.
How it sings against the
turquoise ironwork.

Pastel Flower Power by Kaffe Fassett
The raspberry pink of the Palladian House is perfection as a setting for
my *Pastel Flower Power* – a quilt designed with these colours in mind.

Red Flower Power by Kaffe Fassett
My *Red Flower Power* quilt looks unexpectedly at home against the verdigris metal gate and the warm walls of the Portmeirion Town Hall.

Incredible Stripes by Sally Davis
Who would have thought that the brightness of *Incredible Stripes* would look so perfect in the oriental garden. It harmonizes so well with the red bridge I think they should keep it there permanently.

Gold Italian Tiles by Kaffe Fassett
This glowing yellow tower made me choose this palette for *Gold Italian Tiles*. It is a thrill for me to see it in the setting it was made for.

Summer Tumbling Blocks by Liza Prior Lucy
Liza's quilt showcases the debut collection of
Brandon Mably fabrics. The cheerful pastels speak
to the charming tones of these village buildings.

Autumn Daze by Pauline Smith
Pauline's *Autumn Daze* glows on this winter
beech hedge. A beautiful feature of Portmeirion
is the many classical fountains and statues.

Two Up Two Down by Brandon Mably
How perfect Brandon's child's quilt looks with Portmeirion's equally colourful buildings.

Tulips by Pauline Smith
Pauline's *Tulips* quilt looking jaunty against one of my favourite ironwork windows.

Hearts And Gizzards by Kaffe Fassett
How cool and creamy my *Hearts And Gizzards* quilt looks on the blue and white staircase with its yellow carved details. Another vintage quilt pattern I have wanted to do for some years.

Kim McLean: A Quilter's Story

ABOVE: Kim McLean in her workroom

Bright, cheerful colours are completely joyous to me, perhaps because I was born in the tropics, in Indonesia, although I have called Australia home for most of my life. I live on Sydney's North Shore with my husband Ross and daughter Casey and an old cat. I think I'm a person of contrasts. Whilst strong vibrant colours appeal to me in artistic designs, my home environment is calm and sedate. Home in Sydney is rather neutral and our holiday home by the beach in Mykonos is white in contrast to the azure blue sea outside the windows. The colours in both homes come from vibrant pottery, flowers, paintings and of course the garden. I mainly dress in sedate navy, black and white but I do enjoy wearing crazy shoes and accessories. I'm a clean freak, but have hobbies that generally produce a messy clutter. Just as well I have a dedicated work room with fabrics, patterns and threads all over the place. Plenty of cleaning up required at the conclusion of a project. I tend to focus on one project at a time, but have many jumbled ideas in my head in various stages of development.

When I was quite young, my mother had a cupboard full of interesting knick-knacks; beads, colourful threads by the hundred, buttons and embroidery fabrics. I taught myself to do sampler stitches from a book, and my love for embroidery must have started then. I think I'm a crafts person from way back, I seem to have a need to have something to do in my hands. Constant fiddling during my very early years actually led to several accidents, I managed to pierce my finger with a sewing machine needle, and another time I was playing with the machinery inside the giant family grandfather clock and caused it to crash down on the floor, with me still inside. I'm still fiddling with things now. I love making necklaces with colourful beads; my bead stash almost rivals my fabric collection. I still buy tapestry kits, including Kaffe's and have a collection of cushions made from these kits. I have also spent many afternoons drilling seashells to dress up the driftwood sculptures at our beach house. I make sumptuous tassels for keys too. They're all fun things to do and keep my hands busy.

I love our garden in Sydney. We are blessed with a mild climate, so plants like pansies

BELOW RIGHT: Kim's driftwood sculpture

BELOW: Kim's bead stash

grow in winter. My garden reflects the seasons, pansies in winter and petunias in summer. They are riotous in colour, and against the green, they look happy and bright. I've never had a monotone garden, although perhaps it would be rather glamorous to have one. Sometimes, I have the intention of ordering all the plants in one colour, but as soon as I arrive at the nursery, that thought goes out the window. I'm drawn to the most colourful flowers. I also love the fragrance of the garden throughout the year. At the moment, our daphnes are all out and the scent is heavenly. Earlier, violets were in bloom and the perfume is fantastic when the sun warms the plants each morning. In summer, gardenias rule by the hundreds and the fragrance is overpowering. Competing in the perfume stakes are the tutti frutti scents of the port wine magnolia and stephanotis growing down by the front gate arbour. The fragrances wafting through my work room windows are also part of my inspiration.

I started quilting during the early 1990's when I came across an interesting quilt store near home selling Liberty fabrics. I didn't really know much about quilts then, but went to the store to buy the Liberty fabrics to make Casey's smocked dresses; she was then about 6 years old. During one of those shopping expeditions, I bought a pattern for making doll's quilts. It made absolutely no sense as it was written for template-free machine sewing and I knew nothing about this method. Somehow I worked through it and produced some dinky Amish quilts in Liberty and pastel fabrics. It was not a good look. The quilting tutor at the fabric store suggested I should do a beginner's class. That class really opened up Pandora's Box, and within two years, I had a fabric stash like my life depended on it and had managed to complete two quilts that won Best of Show quilts at the Sydney Quilt show. I also bought quilting publications by the shelf full. My favourite books even now are those produced by the American Quilt Study groups, where each state produced a book with stories of the quilters and the quilts they had made. There were so many beautiful photographs of these antique quilts, I wanted to make them all, especially the appliqué ones. Whilst I could easily draft the pieced quilts, appliqué seemed daunting as I'd never

ABOVE: Kim's *New York Beauty* quilt

BELOW LEFT: Kim's early appliqué quilt

BELOW: Pansies

ABOVE: Kim's mum's ginger jar

BELOW: Kim's *Mary Mannakee* quilt

BELOW RIGHT: Detail

done any creative drawing. I'm a pharmacist by training, so it is second nature to be accurate and rather pedantic. Artistic free form designing seemed to be outside my capabilities. Out of desperation, I started to draw simple figures and found that it wasn't that hard after all. Over the years, this aspect of my designing skill set has improved, but my drawing capability will probably always be somewhat limited. It is however sufficient to draft the naïve appliqué quilts that I enjoy making.

A lot of inspiration for my quilts is around me. Mostly I find it around the house; the flowers in the gardens and also the beautiful multi-coloured parrots who visit each day. I also get inspiration from traveling with my family both within Australia and overseas. Southern France and Italy are exhilarating places to visit. The colours and vibrant light in spring and summer constantly provide inspiration. I love pottery, and I was fortunate enough to have inherited my mother's antique Oriental vases and ginger jars. I've used those as a starting point whenever there is a pot or vase that has to be drawn in the appliqué design. Naïve pottery is another source of inspiration. We have collected many crockery pieces from Italy with whimsical, naïve designs in strong colours. I like to incorporate a touch of the whimsical in my quilt designs like those in the antique quilts.

These days I most enjoy using traditional quilt designs and recasting them in the vibrant fabrics that Kaffe has designed. The quilts I have made using his fabrics look happy and

joyous. People smile when they see them. The first quilt I made with my limited number of Kaffe Fassett fabrics was "Flower Pots". I used some pastel striped fabrics as the background and it looked gorgeous when viewed in "real life" but less so in photographs due to lack of contrast. Had I more fabric variety in my stash at the time, the result would have been better. I learnt something here; establish a good range of fabrics, not necessarily big in yards, but plenty of variety. Now, my Kaffe fabrics collection has increased a hundred fold and I'm much happier working on the quilts. There is nothing like looking at baskets full of colourful fabrics to put a smile on your face and stimulate interesting designs!

I enjoy all aspects of quilting, from the drafting to the finishing of the quilt, but the part I love most would be the cutting of the fabrics and assembling the different prints into a harmonious design that feels right and pleases the eye. For me, handling colours feels quite natural and I don't think I agonize over it very much. Sometimes placing incongruous colours together makes the quilt. The lesson here is, don't be afraid to experiment. People have asked me if I would make pictorial quilts, but I don't have the yearning to do this. Perhaps that type of expression was satisfied in me ages ago when I did a photography course. I enjoy all aspects of traditional quilts too much to change direction, especially now when fabric designers like Kaffe are constantly opening new avenues for me to keep re-inventing these old classics.

ABOVE: Hand painted vase

BELOW: Kim's *Basket Medallion* quilt

BELOW LEFT: Detail

Red Flower Power Quilt ★★

KAFFE FASSETT

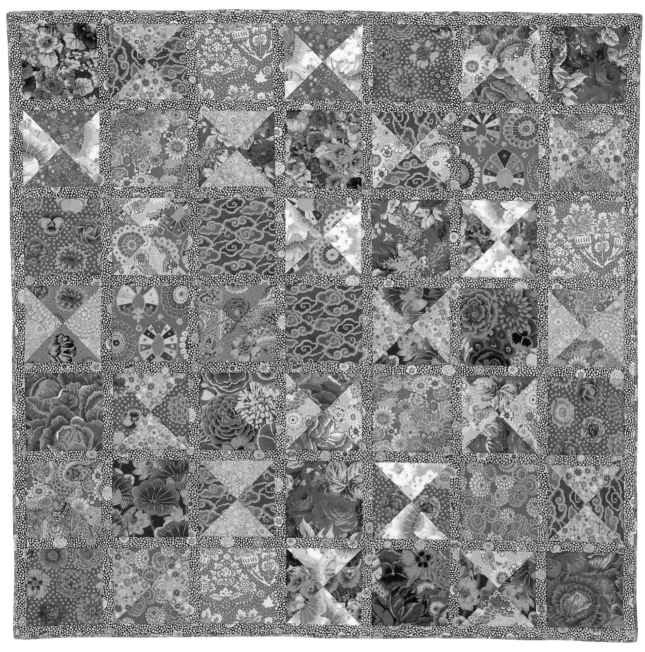

I wanted a simple large scale quilt to show off our new upscale florals. Doing this in two colourways shows you how adaptable these ideas are. Try one in a green or blue palette as well as the pastel version on page 59.

SIZE OF QUILT
The finished quilt will measure approx. 85½in × 85½in (217.25cm × 217.25cm).

MATERIALS
Patchwork Fabrics:

FLOATING FLOWERS
Scarlet	GP56SC: ½yd (45cm)

GUINEA FLOWER
Green	GP59GN: 2⅛yds (2m)

PAISLEY JUNGLE
Green	GP60GN: ½yd (45cm)

BEKAH
Magenta	GP69MG: ½yd (45cm)

STENCIL
Scarlet	GP79SC: ½yd (45cm)

TURKISH DELIGHT
Red	GP81RD: ½yd (45cm)

Block Assembly Diagrams

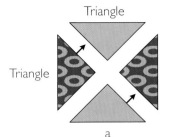
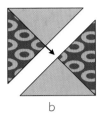

Triangle

Triangle

a   b   c

CLOUDS

Red	GP86RD: ¾yd (70cm)
STAR FLOWER	
Celadon	GP88CE: ½yd (45cm)
Red	GP88RD: ½yd (45cm)
ASIAN CIRCLES	
Green	GP89GN: ½yd (45cm)
Tomato	GP89TM: ½yd (45cm)
BIG BLOOMS	
Red	GP91RD: ¾yd (70cm)
Turquoise	GP91TQ: ½yd (45cm)
MILLEFIORE	
Green	GP92GN: ½yd (45cm)
LAKE BLOSSOMS	
Green	GP93GN: ½yd (45cm)
Red	GP93RD: ½yd (45cm)
CABBAGE PATCH	
Magenta	GP94MG: ½yd (45cm)
TALL HOLLYHOCKS	
Pink	PJ16PK: ½yd (45cm)
LILAC ROSE	
Scarlet	PJ17SC: ¾yd (70cm)

Backing Fabric: 6¾yds (6.2m)
We suggest these fabrics for backing:
BEKAH Magenta, GP69MG
BIG BLOOMS Red, GP91RD
CABBAGE PATCH Magenta, GP94MG

Binding:
ASIAN CIRCLES
Tomato   GP89TM: ¾yd (70cm)

Batting:
93in × 93in (236.5cm × 236.5cm).

Quilting Thread:
Toning hand and machine quilting threads.

PATCH SHAPES
Traditional hourglass blocks, pieced using 1 triangle patch shape (cut to size), are alternated with a square patch shape (cut to size). The blocks and squares are interspaced with sashing (cut to size).

CUTTING OUT
Cut the fabric in the order stated to prevent waste. Cut the Triangles first, then trim and use leftover strips for Squares where appropriate.
Triangles: Cut 11¾in (29.75cm) strips across the width of the fabric. Each strip will give you 12 patches per full width. Cut 11¾in (29.75cm) squares, then cut each square twice diagonally to make 4 triangles. This will ensure the long side of the triangle will not have a bias edge. Note: do not move the patches until both diagonals have been cut. Cut 12 in GP88CE, GP89GN, GP93GN, 8 in GP86RD, GP92GN, 4 in GP56SC, GP60GN, GP81RD, GP88RD, GP89TM, GP91RD, GP91TQ, GP93RD, GP94MG, PJ16PK and PJ17SC.
Squares: Cut 11in (28cm) strips across the width of the fabric. Each strip will give you 3 patches per full width. Cut 11in (28cm) squares. Cut 4 in GP91RD, 3 in GP69MG, GP79SC, PJ17SC, 2 in GP81RD, GP86RD, GP89TM, GP94MG, PJ16PK, 1 in GP56SC and GP93RD.
Sashing: Cut 33 strips 2in (5cm) wide across the width of the fabric in GP59GN. Join strips as necessary and cut 2 sashing strips 2in × 86in (5cm × 218.5cm) 8 sashing strips 2in × 83in (5cm × 211cm) and 42 sashing strips 2in × 11in (5cm × 28cm)

Binding: Cut 9 strips 2½in (6.5cm) wide across the width of the fabric in GP89TM.

Backing: Cut 2 pieces 40in × 93in (101.5cm × 236.5cm), 2 pieces 40in ×14in (101.5cm × 35.5cm) and 1 piece 14in × 14in (35.5cm × 35.5cm) in backing fabric. Note: For a quirky look to the backing you could cut the 14in (35.5cm) square from a different fabric and piece the backing with the contrasting square in the centre.

MAKING THE BLOCKS
Use a ¼in (6mm) seam allowance

Quilting Diagram

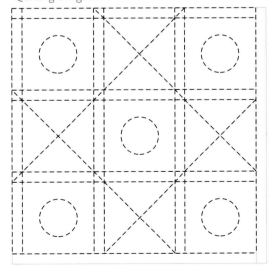

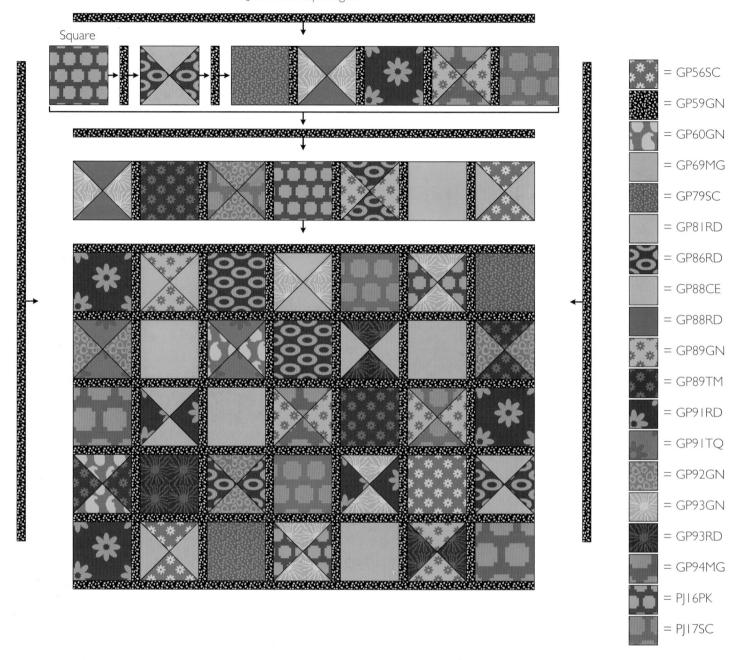

Square

= GP56SC
= GP59GN
= GP60GN
= GP69MG
= GP79SC
= GP81RD
= GP86RD
= GP88CE
= GP88RD
= GP89GN
= GP89TM
= GP91RD
= GP91TQ
= GP92GN
= GP93GN
= GP93RD
= GP94MG
= PJ16PK
= PJ17SC

throughout. Using the quilt assembly diagram as a guide for fabric placement make 24 hourglass blocks as shown in block assembly diagram a and b. The finished block can be seen in diagram c.

MAKING THE QUILT
Arrange the blocks into 7 rows, alternating with the Squares and separated by the short sashing

strips. Join blocks, Squares and sashing strips to form 7 rows. Interspace the rows with the 2in × 83in (5cm × 211cm) sashing strips and join as shown in the quilt assembly diagram. Finally add a 2in × 86in (5cm × 218.5cm) sashing strip to each side to complete the quilt.

FINISHING THE QUILT
Press the quilt top. Seam the backing pieces

using a ¼in (6mm) seam allowance to form a piece approx. 93in × 93in (236.5cm × 236.5cm). Layer the quilt top, batting and backing and baste together (see page 138). Using toning thread machine quilt in the ditch as shown in the quilting diagram, the circles in the centre of each Square are hand quilted, again using toning thread. Trim the quilt edges and attach the binding (see page 139).

Pastel Flower Power Quilt ★★

Kaffe Fassett

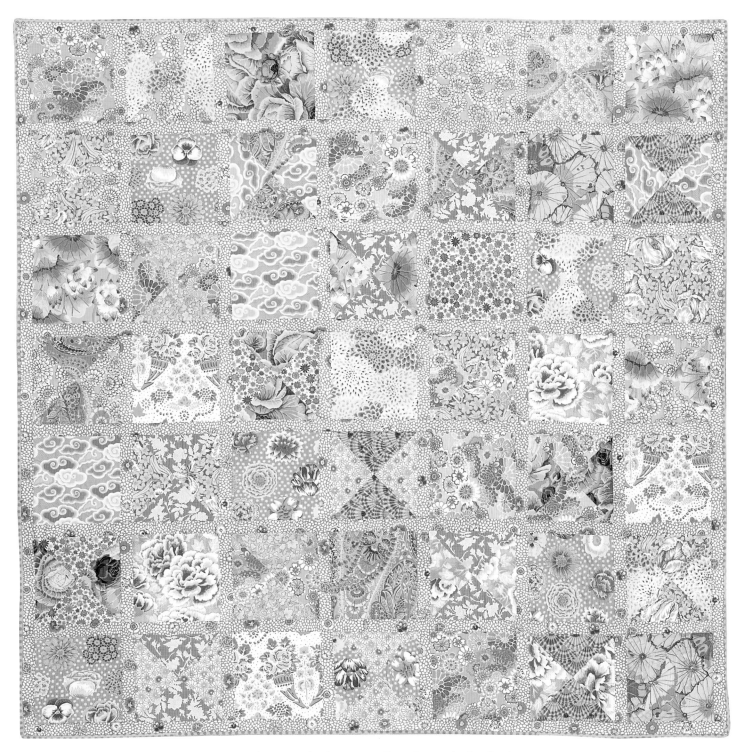

Many vintage Dutch quilts use this simple to make layout and it always looks fresh to me.
Of course I knew these lush pastels would be right at home here in Portmeirion.

SIZE OF QUILT
The finished quilt will measure approx.
85½in × 85½in (217.25cm × 217.25cm).

MATERIALS
Patchwork Fabrics:
LOTUS LEAF
Jade   GP29JA: ½yd (45cm)
KIMONO
Pink/Orange   GP33PO: ½yd (45cm)
DAHLIA BLOOMS
Spring   GP54SP: ½yd (45cm)
FLOATING FLOWERS
Pink   GP56PK: ½yd (45cm)
PAPER FANS
Yellow   GP57YE: ½yd (45cm)
GUINEA FLOWER
Mauve   GP59MV: 2⅛yds (2m)
PAISLEY JUNGLE
Tangerine   GP60TN: ½yd (45cm)
SILHOUETTE ROSE
Pink   GP77PK: ½yd (45cm)
STENCIL
Cream   GP79CM: ½yd (45cm)
DAISY
Cream   GP80CM: ½yd (45cm)
CLOUDS
Duck Egg   GP86DE: ½yd (45cm)
STAR FLOWER
Pastel   GP88PT: ½yd (45cm)
ASIAN CIRCLES
Pink   GP89PK: ½yd (45cm)
Yellow   GP89YE: ½yd (45cm)
BIG BLOOMS
Pink   GP91PK: ¾yd (70cm)
LAKE BLOSSOMS
Yellow   GP93YE: ½yd (45cm)
CABBAGE PATCH
Yellow   GP94YE: ½yd (45cm)
TULIP
Yellow   PJ14YE: ½yd (45cm)
IVY
Pink   PJ19PK: ½yd (45cm)

Backing Fabric: 6¾yds (6.2m)
We suggest these fabrics for backing:
ASIAN CIRCLES Pink, GP89PK
BIG BLOOMS Pink, GP91PK
TULIP Yellow, PJ14YE

Binding:
SPOT
Yellow   GP70YE: ¾yd (70cm)

Batting:
93in × 93in (236.5cm × 236.5cm).

Quilting Thread:
Toning machine quilting threads.

PATCH SHAPES
See Red Flower Power Quilt instructions.

CUTTING OUT
Cut the fabric in the order stated to prevent waste. Cut the Triangles first, then trim and use leftover strips for Squares where appropriate.
Triangles: Cut 11¾in (29.75cm) strips across the width of the fabric. Each strip will give you 12 patches per full width. Cut 11¾in (29.75cm) squares, then cut each square twice diagonally to make 4 triangles. This will ensure the long side of the triangle will not have a bias edge. Note: do not move the patches until both diagonals have been cut. Cut 10 in GP77PK, 8 in GP54SP, GP56PK, GP60TN, GP80CM, PJ14YE, 6 in GP57YE, GP91PK, GP94YE, 4 in GP33PO, GP86DE, GP88PT, GP89PK, GP89YE, GP93YE and PJ19PK.
Squares: Cut 11in (28cm) strips across the width of the fabric. Each strip will give you 3 patches per full width. Cut 11in (28cm) squares. Cut 4 in GP91PK, 3 in GP79CM, 2 in GP29JA, GP33PO, GP86DE, GP89PK, GP89YE, GP93YE, 1 in GP54SP, GP56PK, GP60TN, GP88PT, GP94YE and PJ14YE.
Sashing: Cut 33 strips 2in (5cm) wide across the width of the fabric in GP59MV. Join strips as necessary and cut 2 sashing strips 2in × 86in (5cm × 218.5cm) 8 sashing strips 2in × 83in (5cm × 211cm) and 42 sashing strips 2in × 11in (5cm × 28cm)

Binding: Cut 9 strips 2½in (6.5cm) wide across the width of the fabric in GP70YE.

Backing: Cut 2 pieces 40in × 93in (101.5cm × 236.5cm), 2 pieces 40in × 14in (101.5cm × 35.5cm) and 1 piece 14in × 14in (35.5cm × 35.5cm) in backing fabric. Note: For a quirky look to the backing you could cut the 14in (35.5cm) square from a different fabric and piece the backing with the contrasting square in the centre.

MAKING THE BLOCKS
See Red Flower Power Quilt instructions.

MAKING THE QUILT
See Red Flower Power Quilt instructions.

FINISHING THE QUILT
Press the quilt top. Seam the backing pieces using a ¼in (6mm) seam allowance to form a piece approx. 93in × 93in (236.5cm × 236.5cm). Layer the quilt top, batting and backing and baste together (see page 138). Using toning thread machine quilt in the ditch in all the major block and sashing seams. Then free motion quilt in the squares and triangles following the forms of the fabric motifs. Trim the quilt edges and attach the binding (see page 139).

Quilt Assembly Diagram

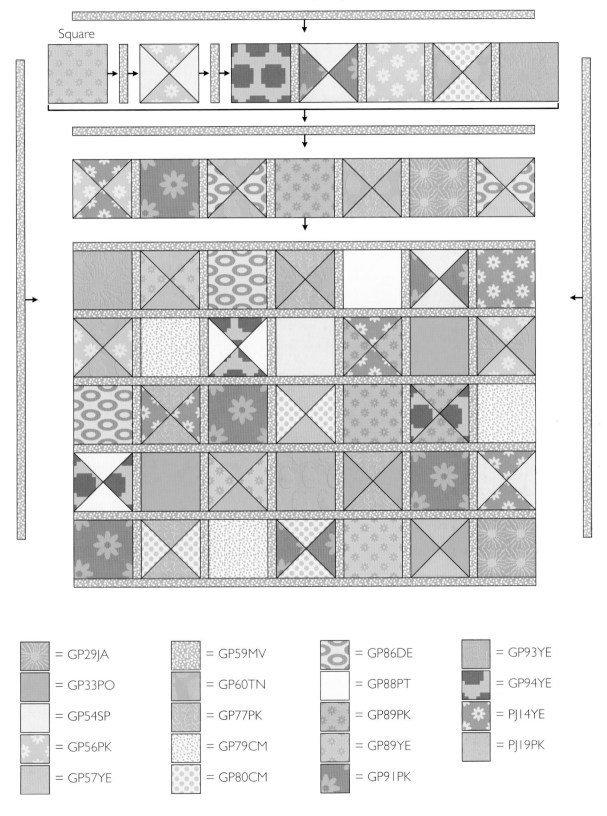

Square

= GP29JA = GP59MV = GP86DE = GP93YE

= GP33PO = GP60TN = GP88PT = GP94YE

= GP54SP = GP77PK = GP89PK = PJ14YE

= GP56PK = GP79CM = GP89YE = PJ19PK

= GP57YE = GP80CM = GP91PK

Jiggery Pokery Quilt ★★

KAFFE FASSETT

I spotted a vintage quilt on ebay in red, white, black and navy, which showed off the ingenious, simple two block layout.

SIZE OF QUILT
The finished quilt will measure approx.
90in x 96in (228.5cm x 244cm).

MATERIALS
Patchwork Fabrics:
FLOATING FLOWERS
Pink   GP56PK: ¾yd (70cm)
Scarlet   GP56SC: ⅝yd (60cm)
GUINEA FLOWER
Apricot   GP59AP: ⅝yd (60cm)

SPOT
Duck Egg   GP70DE: ⅝yd (60cm)
Fuchsia   GP70FU: ⅝yd (60cm)
Gold   GP70GD: ½yd (45cm)
Green   GP70GN: ⅜yd (35cm)
Ice   GP70IC: ⅝yd (60cm)
Lilac   GP70LI: ½yd (45cm)
Magenta   GP70MG: ⅛yd (15cm)
Mint   GP70MT: ⅝yd (60cm)
Pink   GP70PK: ⅞yd (80cm)
Red   GP70RD: ⅜yd (35cm)

Taupe   GP70TA: ⅜yd (35cm)
Tomato   GP70TM: ½yd (45cm)
Turquoise   GP70TQ: ¾yd (70cm)
SILHOUETTE ROSE
Duck Egg   GP77DE: 1⅜yds (1.5m)
Pink   GP77PK: ½yd (45cm)
Wine   GP77WN: ⅝yd (60cm)
ANENOME
Pink   GP78PK: ⅝yd (60cm)
STENCIL
Gold   GP79GD: ½yd (45cm)

TULIP
Yellow   PJ14YE: ⅜yd (35cm)
WOVEN CHECK
Fuchsia   WCHFU: ⅜yd (35cm)
Mint   WCHMT: ½yd (45cm)
Pink   WCHPK: ½yd (45cm)
WOVEN MULTI STRIPE
Ivory   WMSIV: ¾yd (70cm)

Backing Fabric: 8¾yds (8m)
We suggest these fabrics for backing:
WOVEN CHECK Mint, WCHMT or Pink,
WCHPK.

Binding:
SILHOUETTE ROSE
Wine   GP77WN: ⅞yd (80cm)

Batting:
98in × 104in (249cm × 264cm).

Quilting Thread:
Toning hand or machine quilting thread.

Templates:

L   S   V   W   X

PATCH SHAPES

A combination of large 4 patch blocks
pieced using 1 square patch (Template S) and
half square triangle blocks pieced using 1
large triangle patch (Template L) make up the
centre of this lively quilt (both blocks finish to
6in (15.25cm)). The blocks are 'straight set'
into rows. The quilt centre is then surrounded
with a pieced border of small 4 patch blocks
made with a second square patch (Template
V). These 4 patch blocks are set 'on point'
using a medium triangle patch (Templates W)
for the border edges and a small triangle
patch (Template X) for the border ends.

CUTTING OUT

Cut the fabric in the order stated to prevent
waste. Cut the large patches first, then trim
and use leftover strips for smaller patches
where appropriate.
Template L: Cut 6⅞in (17.5cm) strips across
the width of the fabric. Each strip will give
you 10 triangles per full width. Cut 19 in
GP70PK, 12 in GP56PK, 10 in GP70FU, 8 in
GP56SC, GP59AP, GP70DE, GP70IC,
GP70TQ, GP78PK, PJ14YE, WMSIV, 7 in
GP70MT, GP77WN, 6 in GP70GD, GP70LI,

GP70RD, GP70TA, GP70TM, GP77PK,
WCHFU, WCHMT, WCHPK, 5 in GP70GN
and 4 in GP79GD.
Template W: Cut 7¼in (18.5cm) strips
across the width of the fabric. Each strip will
give you 20 triangles per full width. Cut 7¼in
(18.5cm) squares, cut each square twice
diagonally to form 4 triangles using the
template as a guide, this will ensure that the
long side of the triangle will not have a bias
edge. Note: do not move the patches until
both the diagonals have been cut. Cut 108 in
GP77DE.
Template X: Cut 3⅞in (9.75cm) strips across
the width of the fabric. Each strip will give
you 20 triangles per full width. Cut 16 in
GP77DE.
Template S: Cut 3½in (9cm) strips across the
width of the fabric. Each strip will give you 11
patches per full width. Cut 32 in GP70PK, 26
in WMSIV, 25 in GP70TQ, 23 in GP70MT, 22
in GP78PK, 20 in GP77PK, 18 in GP56PK, 17
in GP70IC, 16 in GP56SC, GP59AP, 15 in
GP70LI, 13 in GP70FU, WCHPK, 12 in
GP70DE, GP70GD, 11 in GP70TA, GP70TM,
GP77WN, 9 in GP70GN, 8 in GP70MG,
WCHFU, 7 in GP79GD, PJ14YE, 6 in
GP70RD and WCHMT.
Template V: Cut 2⅝in (6.75cm) strips across
the width of the fabric. Each strip will give
you 15 patches per full width. Cut 21 in
GP77WN, 18 in GP56PK, GP70TQ, 17 in
GP79GD, 15 in GP70DE, 14 in GP70TM,
WMSIV, 13 in GP59AP, GP70MT, WCHPK, 12
in GP70GD, GP70IC, 11 in GP56SC,
WCHMT, 8 in GP70FU, GP70LI, GP78PK and
6 in GP70GN.

Binding: Cut 10 strips 2½in (6.5cm) wide
across the width of the fabric in GP77WN.

Backing: Cut 2 pieces 40in × 98in (101.5cm
× 249cm) and 1 piece 25in × 98in (63.5cm ×
249cm) in backing fabric.

MAKING THE BLOCKS
Use a ¼in (6mm) seam allowance
throughout. Using the quilt assembly diagram
as a guide for fabric placement make 91
large 4 patch blocks using the template S
squares as shown in block assembly diagram
a. The finished 4 patch block can be seen in
diagram b. Make 91 half square triangle
blocks using the template L triangles as
shown in diagram c, the finished half square
triangle block can be seen in diagram d. Also
make 58 small 4 patch blocks using the
template V squares and reserve for the
pieced borders.

MAKING THE QUILT
Arrange the blocks into 14 rows of 13
blocks, alternating the 4 patch with the half
square triangle blocks throughout. Join blocks
into rows, then join the rows to form the
quilt centre. Make 2 side borders as shown in
the quilt assembly diagram each using 14
small 4 patch blocks. Use the template W
triangles for the border edges and the
template X triangles to complete the ends of
the borders. Add a pieced border to each
side of the quilt. In the same way make 2
more pieced borders each using 15 small 4
patch blocks and join to the quilt top and
bottom to complete the quilt.

FINISHING THE QUILT
Press the quilt top. Seam the backing pieces
using a ¼in (6mm) seam allowance to form a
piece approx. 98in × 104in (249cm ×
264cm). Layer the quilt top, batting and
backing and baste together (see page 138).
Quilt by hand or machine using toning
thread. Quilt the large 4 patch blocks in the
ditch continuing the lines across the half
square triangle blocks to form a cross hatch
pattern across the centre of the quilt. In the
border quilt the small 4 patch blocks in the
ditch across the centres and around each
block. Trim the quilt edges and attach the
binding (see page 139).

Block Assembly Diagrams

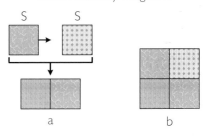

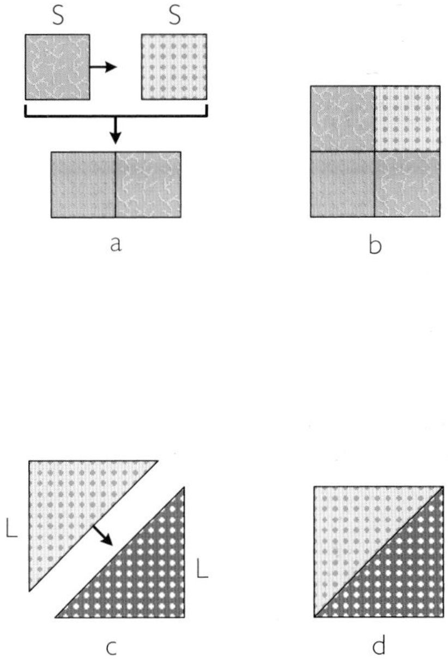

a   b

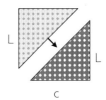

c   d

Quilt Assembly Diagram

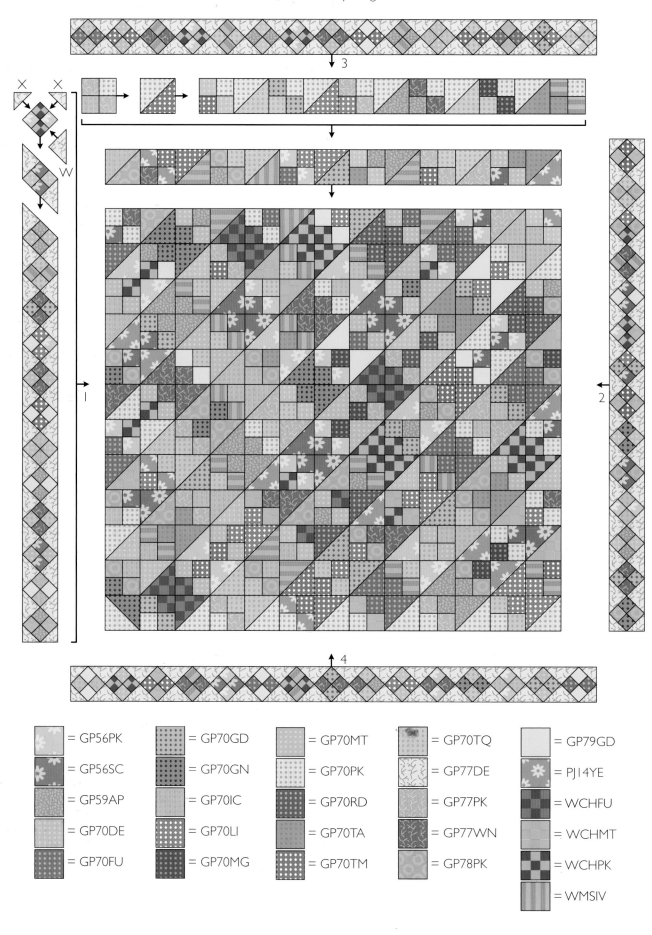

= GP56PK	= GP70GD	= GP70MT	= GP70TQ	= GP79GD
= GP56SC	= GP70GN	= GP70PK	= GP77DE	= PJ14YE
= GP59AP	= GP70IC	= GP70RD	= GP77PK	= WCHFU
= GP70DE	= GP70LI	= GP70TA	= GP77WN	= WCHMT
= GP70FU	= GP70MG	= GP70TM	= GP78PK	= WCHPK
				= WMSIV

Say it with Flowers and Stripes Quilt ★★

MARY MASHUTA

What fun to revamp a scrappy Depression era quilt which only needs 2 templates. Each block requires 4 identical units, but there are pleasing value contrasts between blocks. For my modern twist, I used 6 colourways of a floral and 8 colourways of a stripe to accomplish the same visual impact that quilters used to achieve using their scrapbags.

SIZE OF QUILT
The finished quilt will measure approx.
65in x 78in (165cm x 198cm).

MATERIALS
Patchwork Fabrics:
ASIAN CIRCLES
Dark   GP89DK: ⅝yd (60cm)

Green	GP89GN: ⅝yd (60cm)
Orange	GP89OR: ⅝yd (60cm)
Pink	GP89PK: ¾yd (70cm)
Tomato	GP89TM: ⅝yd (60cm)
Yellow	GP89YE: ⅝yd (60cm)

WOVEN MULTI STRIPE
| Brown | WMSBR: ⅜yd (35cm) |

Fuchsia	WMSFU: ½yd (45cm)
Green	WMSGN: ⅜yd (35cm)
Indigo	WMSIN: ⅜yd (35cm)
Ivory	WMSIV: ⅝yd (60cm)
Purple	WMSPU: ⅜yd (35cm)
Red	WMSRD: ½yd (45cm)
Teal	WMSTE: ½yd (45cm)

Backing Fabric: 5yds (4.6m)
We suggest these fabrics for backing:
BIG BLOOMS Red, GP91RD
ASIAN CIRCLES Tomato, GP89TM
WOVEN MULTI STRIPE Red, WMSRD

Binding:
WOVEN MULTI STRIPE
Red   WMSRD: ⅝yd (60cm)

Batting:
73in × 86in (185.5cm × 218.5cm).

Quilting Thread:
Toning machine quilting thread.

Templates:

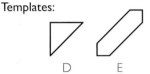

D   E

PATCH SHAPES
The quilt has thirty 4-unit blocks made from mixing six colourway versions of a floral print with eight colourway versions of a stripe. For each block four identical units are made by sewing 2 triangle patch shapes (Template D) to a polygon patch shape (Template E).

CUTTING OUT
Important Information:
Please read carefully before cutting the stripe fabrics.
1. Open out the stripe fabric and cut one layer at a time.
2. Use a gridded ruler to get the first accurate cut across the fabric by lining up the stripe lines with ruler lines and cutting along

the perpendicular edge of the ruler across the fabric width. Keep checking that your stripes are still perpendicular to the ruler edge as you cut. Take time to correct, if necessary. This extra effort is worth it, and a little extra fabric has been allowed for you to 'true up' your stripes.
Template D: Cut 5⅝in (14.25cm) strips across the width of the fabric. Each strip will give you 14 patches per full width. Cut 48 in GP89PK, 40 in GP89DK, GP89GN, GP89OR, GP89TM and 32 in GP89YE.
Template E: Cut 3in (7.75cm) strips across the width of the fabric. Each strip will give

you 4 patches per full width. Cut 24 in WMSIV, 16 in WMSFU, WMSRD, WMSTE, 12 in WMSBR, WMSGN, WMSIN and WMSPU.

Binding: Cut 8½yds (7.8m) of 2½in (6.5cm) wide bias binding in WMSRD.

Backing: Cut 2 pieces 37in × 86in (94cm × 218.5cm) in backing fabric.

MAKING THE QUILT
Use a ¼in (6mm) seam allowance throughout. Using the quilt assembly diagram as a guide for fabric placement make 120

Quilting Diagram

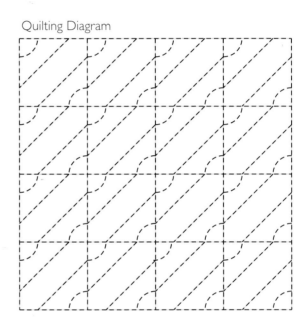

Block Assembly Diagrams

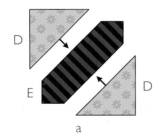

a

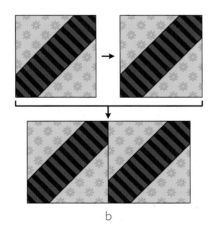

b

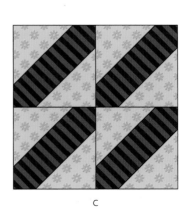

c

Quilt Assembly Diagram

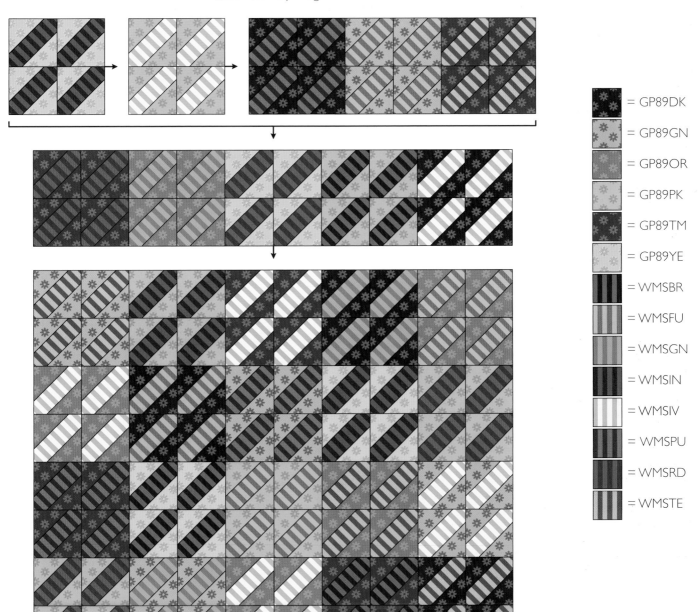

= GP89DK

= GP89GN

= GP89OR

= GP89PK

= GP89TM

= GP89YE

= WMSBR

= WMSFU

= WMSGN

= WMSIN

= WMSIV

= WMSPU

= WMSRD

= WMSTE

units, in sets of 4 identical units, as shown in block assembly diagram a, pressing the seam allowances towards the template E shape. Take 4 identical units and join to form a block as shown in block assembly diagram b. The finished block can be seen in diagram c. Make a total of 30 blocks and lay them out as shown in the quilt assembly diagram. Piece the blocks into 6 rows of 5 units, then join the rows to form the quilt.

FINISHING THE QUILT
Press the quilt top. Seam the backing pieces using a ¼in (6mm) seam allowance to form a piece approx. 73in x 86in (185.5cm x 218.5cm). Layer the quilt top, batting and backing and baste together (see page 138). Refer to the quilting diagram and stitch in the ditch all vertical and horizontal seams using toning machine quilting thread. For the diagonal quilting use a contrasting coloured thread and lengthen the stitch to show off the thread colour. Trim the quilt edges and attach the binding (see page 139).

Pickle Dish Quilt ★★★
KAFFE FASSETT

How I jump every time I see this sprightly design in vintage quilt books. I tried to keep a jolly scrap look to the fabric choices. It needs quite a lot of contrast to show its sparkling form.

SIZE OF QUILT
The finished quilt will measure approx.
67in × 67in (170.25cm × 170.25cm).

MATERIALS
Patchwork and Border Fabrics:
FLOATING FLOWERS
Scarlet   GP56SC: ⅜yd (35cm)
GUINEA FLOWER
Apricot   GP59AP: ⅜yd (35cm)
Blue   GP59BL: ⅜yd (35cm)
Mauve   GP59MV: 1¾yds (1.6m)
SPOT
Fuchsia   GP70FU: ¾yd (70cm)
Lilac   GP70LI: ⅝yd (60cm)
Magenta   GP70MG: ⅝yd (60cm)
Mint   GP70MT: ⅜yd (35cm)
Pink   GP70PK: ⅝yd (60cm)
Purple   GP70PU: ⅜yd (35cm)
Tomato   GP70TM: ½yd (45cm)
ABORIGINAL DOTS
Ivory   GP71IV: ⅜yd (35cm)

Orange   GP71OR: ⅜yd (35cm)
Pink   GP71PK: ⅜yd (35cm)
Sweet Pea   GP71SW: ½yd (45cm)
FLOWER DOT
Grey   GP87GY: ⅝yd (60cm)
Red   GP87RD: ½yd (45cm)
Tan   GP87TN: ½yd (45cm)
ASIAN CIRCLES
Pink   GP89PK: ⅜yd (35cm)
Tomato   GP89TM: ⅜yd (35cm)
WOVEN MULTI STRIPE
Ivory   WMSIV: ⅝yd (60cm)

Backing Fabric: 4½yds (4.1m)
We suggest these fabrics for backing:
ASIAN CIRCLES Tomato, GP89TM
SPOT Lilac, GP70LI
ABORIGINAL DOTS Sweet Pea, GP71SW

Binding:
SPOT
Tomato   GP70TM: ⅝yd (60cm)

Batting:
75in × 75in (190.5cm × 190.5cm).

Quilting Thread:
Toning hand quilting thread.

Templates:

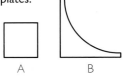

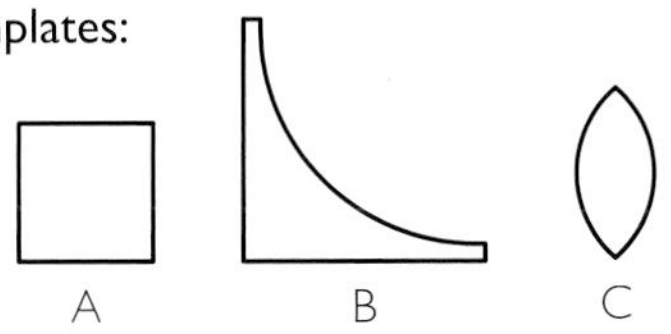

This quilt also uses the Foundation Pattern printed on page 123.

PATCH SHAPES
The traditional pickle dish blocks (finish to 10 inches (25.5cm) square), which make up the centre of this quilt are pieced using a square patch shape (Template A), a curved corner patch shape (Template B), an ellipse patch shape (Template C) and a foundation pieced

Block Assembly Diagrams

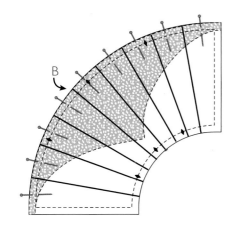

a

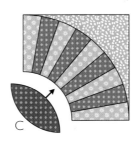

b

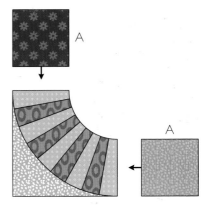

c

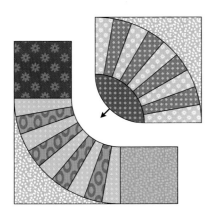

d

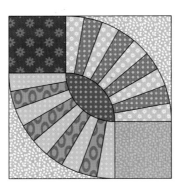

e

f

curved section (Foundation Pattern) made up of 9 'spokes' (2 foundation patterns per block). The blocks are stitched into 'straight set' rows and surrounded with a pieced border using the square patch shape (Template A) and a border strip (cut to size).

CUTTING OUT

Template A: Cut 4in (10.25cm) strips across the width of the fabric. Each strip will give you 10 patches per full width. Cut 20 in GP89TM, 18 in GP89PK, GP59BL, 16 in GP59AP, 14 in GP56SC and GP87GY.

Template B: Cut 7in (17.75cm) strips across the width of the fabric. Each strip will give you 10 patches per full width. Cut 72 in GP59MV.

Template C: Cut 5in (12.75cm) strips across the width of the fabric. Each strip will give you 15 patches per full width. Cut 11 in GP70MG, 9 in GP70LI, 8 in GP70FU and GP70PU.

'Spokes' for Foundation: Cut 4½in (11.5cm) strips across the width of the fabric. Each strip will give you 22 patches per full width. Cut 4½in x 1¾in (11.5cm x 4.5cm) rectangles. Cut 82 in GP87GY, 77 in GP70PK, 59 in GP71SW, 51 in GP87RD, 50 in GP70FU, 49 in GP70TM, 46 in GP87TN, 43 in GP71OR, 38 in GP70MT, 37 in GP70LI, GP71PK, 31 in GP71IV, 28 in GP70MG and 20 in GP70PU.

Border Strips: Cut 4in (10.25cm) strips across the width of the fabric. Each strip will give you 3 strips per full width. Cut 13½in x 4in (34.35cm x 10.25cm) strips. Cut 12 in WMSIV.

Binding: Cut 7 strips 2½in (6.5cm) wide across the width of the fabric in GP70TM.

Backing: Cut 2 pieces 38in x 75in (96.5cm x 190.5cm) in backing fabric.

MAKING THE BLOCKS

The blocks for this quilt are divided into 2 types which are set alternately throughout the quilt. The 2 types can be seen in block assembly diagrams e and f. Type e blocks have dark corner squares (Template A) and the spokes of the foundation pieced section run alternately with light fabric at both ends of the arc, adjacent to the darker corner squares. Type f blocks are the opposite, with light corner squares and the spokes run alternately with dark at both ends of the arc, adjacent to the lighter corner squares. This arrangement of colour and pattern means that where the blocks come together there is always a dark and light spoke adjacent and a four patch at the corners of 2 light and 2 dark squares in the same 2 fabrics.

Foundation Piecing:

The instruction below describes a type e block. For the diagrams RS = Right side, WS = Wrong Side. The foundation papers have a number in each section, this is the order in which pieces are added.

Stage 1: Trace or photocopy then cut out 72 copies of the foundation pattern on page 123 (you may wish to make extra copies for practice). The thinnest 'bank' paper or low quality photocopy paper works well. Using the quilt assembly diagram as a guide for fabric placement, select 5 light and 4 dark 'spoke' rectangles. Take a dark rectangle and a light rectangle place them right sides together. Turn the foundation paper face down and place fabric over section 1 of the paper with the light fabric next to the paper as shown in the foundation piecing stage 1 diagram.

Stage 2: Holding the paper and fabric in place turn the paper over so that the sewing lines are visible. To check the fabric positioning use 2 or 3 pins to secure the fabric along the sewing line ensuring that the fabric edges extend ¼in (6mm) beyond the line between sections 1 and 2. Flip the fabric open to check both section 1 and section 2 will be completely covered by fabric, including all the seam allowance. Holding the paper up to the light is a good way to check. Adjust the fabric positions if necessary, then pin in place ready for stitching. Set your machine to a short stitch, this will perforate the paper and make removal easier later. With the paper upmost stitch on the line between sections 1 and 2, as shown in the stage 2 diagram.

Stage 3: Turn the paper over and open out the 2 fabric rectangles, press without using steam as it can wrinkle the paper.

Stage 4: Fold the foundation paper on the next sewing line, in this case between sections 2 and 3, as shown in the stage 4 diagram.

Stage 5: Trim the fabric to ¼in (6mm) beyond the paper, as shown in the stage 5 diagram.

Stage 6: Take the next rectangle, light in this case, and match to the trimmed edge of the previous fabric, pin along the sewing line and flip it back and check it will cover section 3 once stitched. Stitch on the sewing line between sections 2 and 3, as shown in the stage 6 diagram.

In the same manner as stages 3-6 open out the fabric, press, fold the paper on the next sewing line and trim to ¼in beyond the next sewing line. Add the next rectangle. Keep doing this until all the sections are covered. Trim away any excess fabric to the solid cutting line. Do not remove the paper yet! Make 2 per block, 36 for type e blocks and 36 for type f blocks.

Curved Piecing:

Use a ¼in (6mm) seam allowance throughout. Important Preparation: Lay out all the foundation pieced sections and fill in the template A corner squares making sure that the four patch blocks which will form at the block intersections are in the same fabrics as shown in the quilt assembly diagram as it is crucial to the overall look of the quilt. We recommend using a design wall for this.

Gather all the patches for the first block, 2 foundation pieced sections, 2 template A squares, 2 template B patches and 1 template C patch.

Diagram a: Take a pieced foundation section and a template B curved corner patch and place the right sides together. Carefully match the curved edges by pinning at both ends, then matching the diamond markers and pinning all along the curve. You can make very small clips in the curved edge of the template B patch to ease the matching. Stitch with the paper upmost on the dotted stitching line, open out and press, again without steam.

Diagram b: Add a template C ellipse to the opposite curved edge in the same manner.

Diagram c: Take the second foundation pieced section and join the second template b patch to it as before, then add template A square to each end as shown.

Diagram d: Join the 2 sections together, again carefully matching the curved edges at the diamond markers, stitch and press. Do not remove the paper yet!

Diagrams e and f: These diagrams show the 2 block styles. Make 18 of each type.

MAKING THE QUILT

Arrange the blocks into 6 rows, alternating the block e and block f types throughout. Join the blocks into rows, then join the rows to form the quilt centre as shown in the quilt assembly diagram. Piece the borders using the template A squares and border strips, ensuring that the light and dark pattern in the four patches at the block intersections is continued into the borders. Add the borders as shown in the quilt assembly diagram. Finally, you can remove the papers!

FINISHING THE QUILT
Press the quilt top. Seam the backing pieces using a ¼in (6mm) seam allowance to form a piece approx. 75in x 75in (190.5cm x 190.5cm). Layer the quilt top, batting and backing and baste together (see page 138). Using toning hand quilting thread, quilt ¼in (6mm) inside the seam on the template c ellipses and along the curves of the template b patches. On the foundation sections quilt on the dark 'spokes' offset by ¼in (6mm) to avoid the seam lines. Quilt in the ditch on the four patches at the block intersections. Trim the quilt edges and attach the binding (see page 139).

Foundation Piecing Diagrams

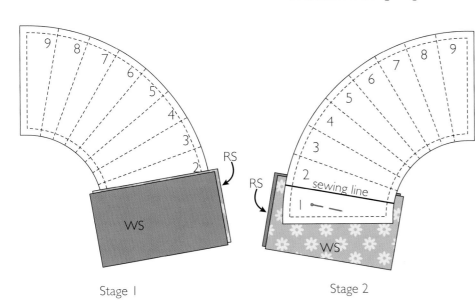

Stage 1

Stage 2

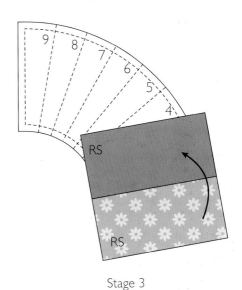

Stage 3

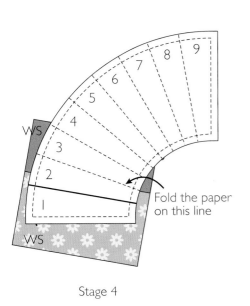

Stage 4

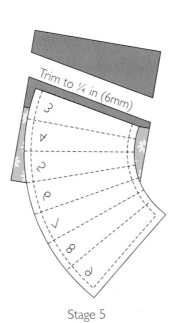

Trim to ¼ in (6mm)

Stage 5

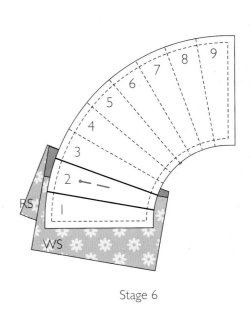

Stage 6

Quilt Assembly Diagram

A Border Strip

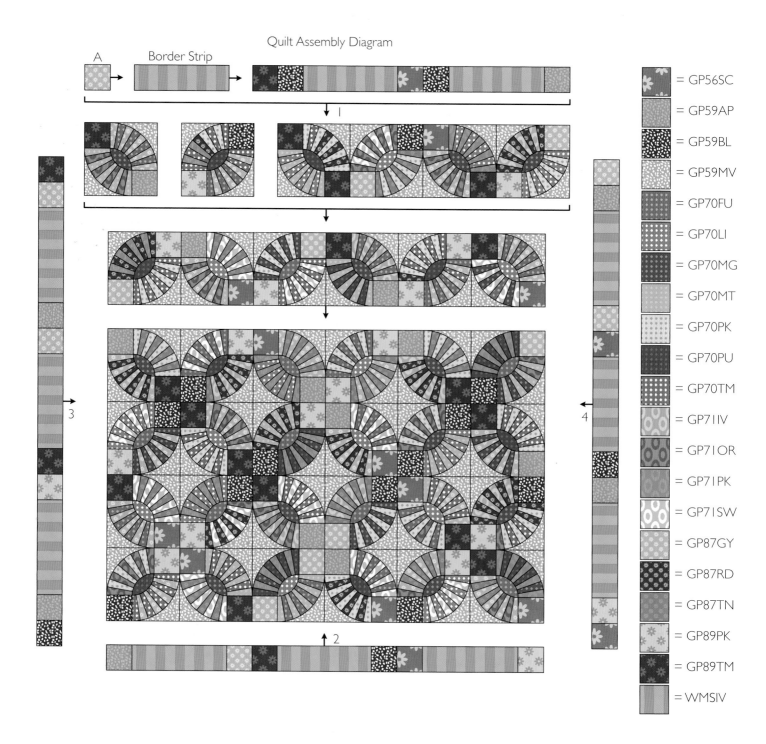

= GP56SC

= GP59AP

= GP59BL

= GP59MV

= GP70FU

= GP70LI

= GP70MG

= GP70MT

= GP70PK

= GP70PU

= GP70TM

= GP71IV

= GP71OR

= GP71PK

= GP71SW

= GP87GY

= GP87RD

= GP87TN

= GP89PK

= GP89TM

= WMSIV

72

Two Up Two Down Quilt ★★

BRANDON MABLY

For me Portmeirion is about the marvellous odd juxtaposition of the buildings with jaunty colours. From sugared almond colours to deep Mediterranean tones. The idea of playing with these happy colours in my own version of a school house quilt fits in a treat.

SIZE OF QUILT
The finished quilt will measure approx.
50in x 44in (127cm x 112cm).

MATERIALS
Patchwork and Sashing Fabrics:
DAHLIA BLOOMS
Succulent   GP54SC: ⅜yd (35cm)
FLOATING FLOWERS
Scarlet   GP56SC: ⅛yd (15cm)

GUINEA FLOWER
Pink   GP59PK: ⅛yd (15cm)
SPOT
Fuchsia   GP70FU: ⅛yd (15cm)
Periwinkle   GP70PE: ⅛yd (15cm)
Purple   GP70PU: ⅛yd (15cm)
PERSIMMON
Orange   GP74OR: ¼yd (25cm)
LICHEN
Lilac   GP76LI: ¼yd (25cm)

Rust   GP76RU: ⅛yd (15cm)
SILHOUETTE ROSE
Pink   GP77PK: ¼yd (25cm)
WINDING FLORAL
Jade   GP85JA: ¼yd (25cm)
CLOUDS
Duck Egg   GP86DE:1¼yds (1.15m)
FLOWER DOT
Cobalt   GP87CB: ⅛yd (15cm)
Moss   GP87MS: ⅛yd (15cm)

Block Assembly Diagrams

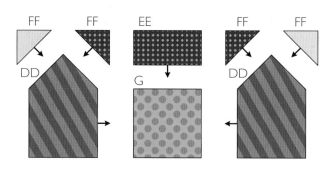

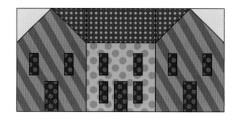

a

b

Red   GP87RD: ⅛yd (15cm)
Tan   GP87TN: ¼yd (25cm)
STARFLOWER
Celadon   GP88CD: ⅜yd (35cm)
ASIAN CIRCLES
Orange   GP89OR: ¼yd (25cm)
DIAGONAL STRIPE
Pink   GP90PK: ¼yd (25cm)
BEGONIA LEAVES
Gold   PJ18GD: ¼yd (25cm)
IVY
Lime   PJ19LM: ¼yd (25cm)

Backing Fabric: 3¼yds (3m)
We suggest these fabrics for backing:
RIPPLE Lavender, BM02LV
WAVES Lipstick, BM04LP
SPOT Periwinkle, GP70PE

Binding:
DIAGONAL STRIPE
Pink   GP90PK: ½yd (45cm)

Batting:
58in × 52in (147.5cm × 132cm).

Quilting Thread:
Toning machine quilting thread.
You Will Also Need:
Non–sew adhesive web for appliqué.

Templates:

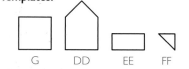

G   DD   EE   FF

This quilt also uses the appliqué shapes on page 130.

PATCH SHAPES
This version of the traditional schoolhouse block is made using 1 square patch (Template G, 1 lozenge patch (Template DD), 1 rectangle (Template EE) and 1 triangle (Template FF). The doors and windows are appliquéd using adhesive web, we suggest using the non–sew type as the shapes are quite small, however instructions for both sew and non–sew adhesive web can be found in the Patchwork Knowhow section in the back of the book. The blocks are interspaced and surrounded with sashing to complete the quilt.

CUTTING OUT
Cut the fabric in the order stated to prevent waste. Use leftover strips for subsequent templates trimming as necessary.
Sashing: Cut 12 strips 2½in (6.25cm) wide across the width of the fabric in GP86DE. Join strips as necessary and cut 2 vertical sashing strips 2½in × 50½in (6.25cm × 128.25cm), 7 horizontal sashing strips 2½in × 40½in (6.25cm × 102.75cm) and 12 sashing strips 2½in × 6½in (6.25cm × 16.5cm).
Template DD: Cut 4½in (11.5cm) strips across the width of the fabric. Each strip will give you 6 patches per full width. Cut 10 in GP88CD, 6 in GP54SC, GP85JA, GP90PK, 4 in PJ18GD, 2 in GP76LI and PJ19LM.
Template G: Cut 4½in (11.5cm) strips across the width of the fabric. Cut 4 in GP77PK, GP89OR, 3 in GP74OR, 2 in GP76LI, GP87TN, 1 in GP54SC, GP88CD and PJ19LM.
Template FF: Cut 2⅞in (7.25cm) strips across the width of the fabric. Each strip will give you 26 patches per full width. Cut 36 in GP86DE, 8 in GP70FU, 6 in GP56SC, GP59PK, GP70PE, GP87RD and 4 in GP76RU.
Template EE: Cut 2½in (6.25cm) strips across the width of the fabric. Cut 4 in GP70FU, 3 in GP56SC, GP59PK, GP70PE,

GP87RD and 2 in GP76RU.
Appliqué Shapes: Trace 54 doors and 144 windows onto the paper side of your adhesive web leaving a ¼in (6mm) gap between the shapes. Roughly cut out the shapes about ⅛in (3mm) outside your drawn line. Bond the shapes to the REVERSE of the fabrics. Bond 21 doors in GP70PU, GP87CB and 12 in GP87MS. Bond 56 windows in GP70PU, GP87CB and 32 in GP87MS.

Binding: Cut 7 strips 2½in (6.5cm) wide across the width of the fabric in GP90PK.

Backing: Cut 1 piece 40in × 52in (101.5cm × 132cm) and 1 piece 19in × 52in (48.25cm × 132cm) in backing fabric.

MAKING THE BLOCKS
Use a ¼in (6mm) seam allowance throughout. Use the quilt assembly diagram as a guide to fabric placement. Piece 18 schoolhouse blocks, as shown in block assembly diagram a. The finished block can be seen in diagram b. This also shows the positions of the appliqué doors and windows. Full instructions for using adhesive web for appliqué can be found in the Patchwork Knowhow section on page 137. Remove the backing paper from the appliqué shapes and position carefully as shown in diagram b. The doors should be aligned with the raw edge of the block, so that the bottom ¼in (6mm) will be stitched into the seam when the block is joined to the sashing later. Bond the shapes into place according to the manufacturer's instructions.

MAKING THE QUILT
Arrange the blocks into 6 rows of 3 blocks as shown in the quilt assembly diagram, interspacing the blocks with the short sashing

strips. Join the blocks into rows, then interspace the rows with the horizontal sashing strips and join. Finally add the vertical sashing strips to the sides to complete the quilt.

FINISHING THE QUILT
Press the quilt top. Seam the backing pieces using a ¼in (6mm) seam allowance to form a piece approx. 58in x 52in (147.5cm x 132cm). Layer the quilt top,

batting and backing and baste together (see page 138). Using toning machine quilting thread, stitch in the ditch throughout. Trim the quilt edges and attach the binding (see page 139).

Quilt Assembly Diagram

= GP54SC
= GP56SC
= GP59PK
= GP70FU
= GP70PE
= GP70PU
= GP74OR
= GP76LI
= GP76RU
= GP77PK
= GP85JA
= GP86DE
= GP87CB
= GP87MS
= GP87RD
= GP87TN
= GP88CD
= GP89OR
= GP90PK
= PJ18GD
= PJ19LM

Cutting Corners Quilt ★★★

KAFFE FASSETT

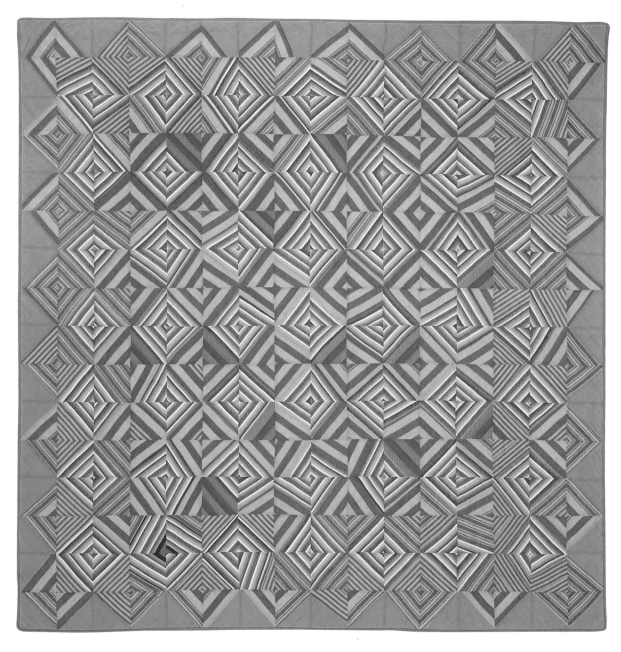

This is the simplest quilt with the least amount of fabrics and is all the better for it. The richness of variation really shows because the palette is so restricted. Of course any two striped fabrics could be used, so do your own look on this fun quilt.

SIZE OF QUILT
The finished quilt will measure approx. 80in x 80in (203cm x 203cm).

MATERIALS
Patchwork Fabrics:
SHOT COTTON
Sky	SC62:	⅜yd (35cm)
Mint	SC65:	1yd (90cm)
Pudding	SC68:	⅜yd (35cm)

WOVEN MULTI STRIPE
Ivory	WMSIV:	3½yds (3.2m)

WOVEN TONE STRIPE
Green	WTSGN:	5yds (4.6m)

Backing Fabric: 6yds (5.5m)
We suggest these fabrics for backing:
SPOT Mint, GP70MT
ABORIGINAL DOTS Ocean, GP71ON
WOVEN MULTI STRIPE Ivory, WMSIV

Binding:
SHOT COTTON
Pudding	SC68:	¾yd (70cm)

Batting:
88in x 88in (223.5cm x 223.5cm).

Quilting Thread:
Toning hand quilting thread.

Templates:

Y

PATCH SHAPES
VERY IMPORTANT: Please read the whole

instruction before starting.

This quilt is great fun to make but a relaxed frame of mind is needed. Don't try to copy it exactly or you might go mad! The block for this quilt is a 5½in (14cm) square (Template Y) which is cut from combinations of fabrics that have been seamed to form a strip. Using a clear plastic template is essential for cutting this quilt. The square is placed 'on point' and is tilted and/or offset from the centre seam within the guidelines on the template to give a 'wonky diamonds' look when the blocks are joined. Try out this technique using some scrap fabrics, you will discover that only a small tilt and/or offset will produce a wonky effect, if the tilt and/or offset is too exaggerated you will not make a diamond when the blocks are combined to form four–patch blocks.

The blocks are combined into four–patch blocks which are joined to form the quilt. The Woven Tone Stripe fabric has 3 widths of stripe, the widest stripe sections are used mainly in the centre and around the outside of the quilt. We recommend cutting the whole quilt before piecing the blocks together, starting with the centre and working out to the edge. We also strongly recommend using a design wall (see glossary) to lay out the blocks as you cut them. That way you can combine your blocks to the best effect. Note: The quilt assembly diagram for this quilt shows the fabric positions accurately but not the tilts/offsets

or stripe widths, refer to the photograph for more help.

CUTTING OUT
These cutting instructions are less formal than usual. The nature of the wonky cutting means everyone's leftovers will look different, so please look at the cutting diagrams with an open mind. The fabric quantities specified are generous, but use your fabric wisely and reuse leftovers to make more available fabric to cut squares.

Fabric WTSGN: Cut 5½in (14cm) strips down the length of the fabric parallel with the selvedge. Try to keep mostly 1 width of stripe to each cut strip.

Fabric WMSIV: Cut 5½in (14cm) strips down the length of the fabric parallel with the selvedge.

Fabrics SC62 and SC68: Cut 1½in (3.75cm) strips across the width of the fabric. Cut 6 in SC68 and 4 in SC62. Join the strips into 2 sets of 5 strips alternating the colours SC68, SC62, SC68, SC62, SC68. Use each of these sets as though they were one fabric.

SC65: Cut 5½in (14cm) strips across the width of the fabric. Join these strips to make lengths to match the strips cut in WTSGN.

Binding: Cut 9 strips 2½in (6.5cm) wide across the width of the fabric in SC68.

Backing: Cut 2 pieces 40in × 88in (101.5cm × 223.5cm), 2 pieces 40in × 9in (101.5cm × 22.75cm) and 1 piece 9in × 9in (22.75cm ×

22.75cm) in backing fabric. Note: For a quirky look to the backing you could cut the 9in (22.75cm) square from a different fabric and piece the backing with the contrasting square in the centre.

MAKING THE BLOCKS
Use a ¼in (6mm) seam allowance throughout and refer to the quilt assembly diagram for fabric combinations. Take the 5½in strips of fabric and join in sets as shown in cutting diagram a.

Make a plastic version of template Y and mark on the tilt and offset guide lines. These are the maximum tilt and offset from the centre seam you should use when cutting your blocks. Place the template on your fabric and tilt and/or offset. Draw around the square and repeat varying the tilts and offsets as shown in diagram a, leaving about 1in (2.5cm) between the squares so that the leftovers will be useable. Cut out sets of 4 squares as shown in diagram b, laying out the sets on a design wall as you go. You can mix up sets to get the best effect, but keep the same stripe width of WTSGN to each set as far as possible.

Don't worry if the leftovers are in smaller pieces, the diagram is just to show the idea. Take the leftover fabric and unpick the centre seams with a seam ripper to separate the two strips. Use the leftovers to piece more fabric sets for more squares as shown in diagram c.

Block Assembly Diagrams

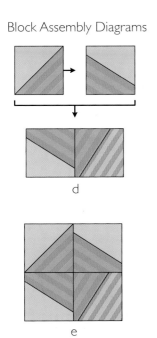

Cutting Diagrams

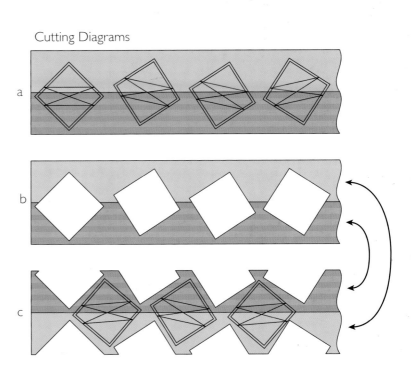

Cut squares in the following combinations of fabric:

SC65/WTSGN: Cut 60 squares
WTSGN/WMSIV: Cut 184 squares
SC62/SC68/WMSIV: Cut 12 squares.

MAKING THE QUILT

Handle your cut blocks carefully as they have bias cut edges and will be stretchy. Lay out the blocks using a design wall. Move your blocks around until you have a pleasing combination, then piece them into four–patch blocks as shown in block assembly diagram d, use plenty of pins to assist in piecing the bias edges. The finished four–patch block can be seen in diagram e. Make 64 four–patch blocks. Join the blocks into 8 rows of 8 blocks. Join the rows to form the quilt.

FINISHING THE QUILT

Press the quilt top. Seam the backing pieces using a ¼in (6mm) seam allowance to form a piece approx. 88in × 88in (223.5cm × 223.5cm). Layer the quilt top, batting and backing and baste together (see page 138). Using toning hand quilting thread, quilt 4 or 5 diagonal lines across each square following the fabric stripes and seams. In the SC65 green border area quilt 'v' shapes of 2 parallel lines in each section, the lines should be about ½in (1.25cm) apart. Trim the quilt edges and attach the binding (see page 139).

Quilt Assembly Diagram

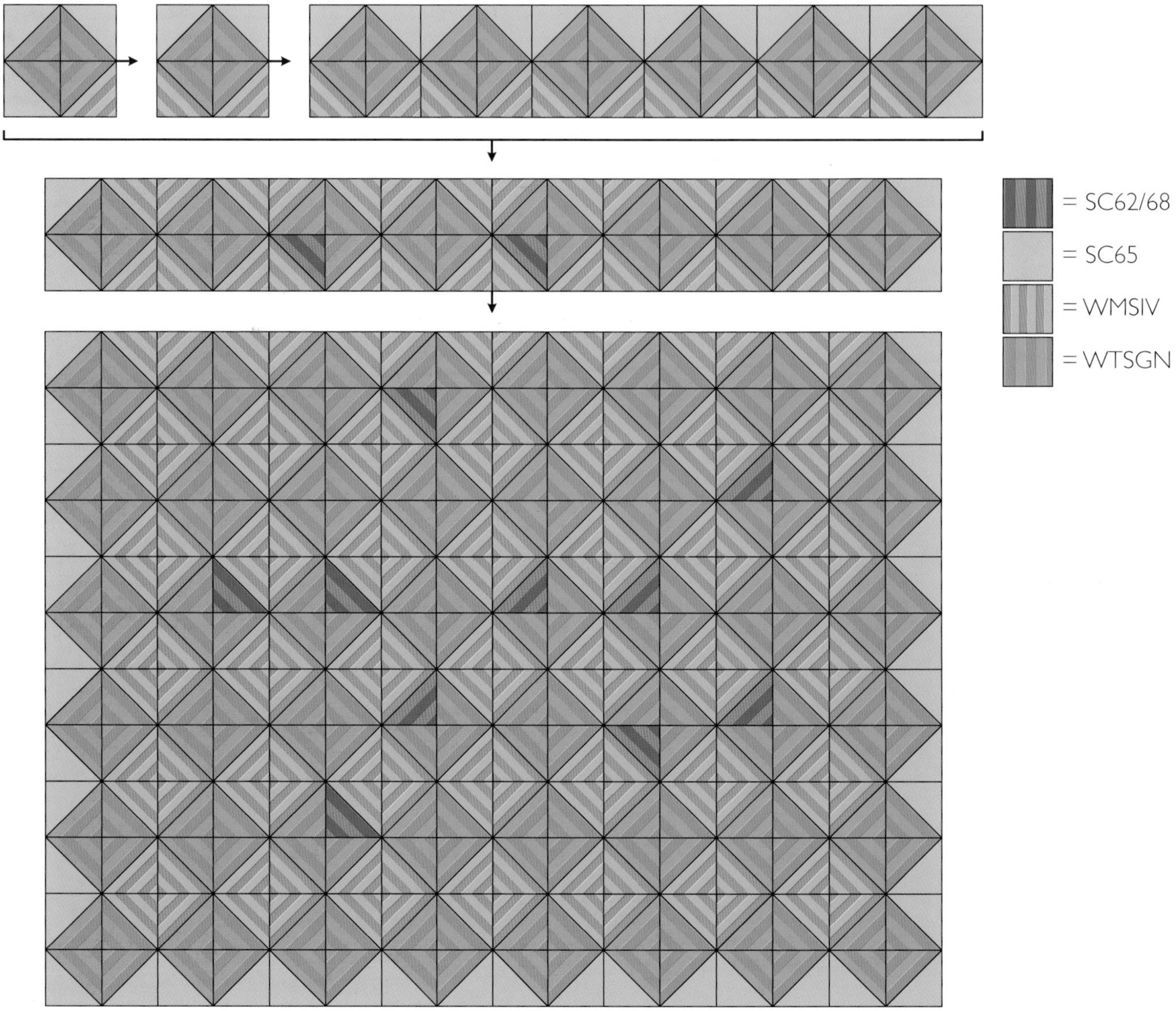

= SC62/68
= SC65
= WMSIV
= WTSGN

Hearts And Gizzards Quilt ★★★

KAFFE FASSETT

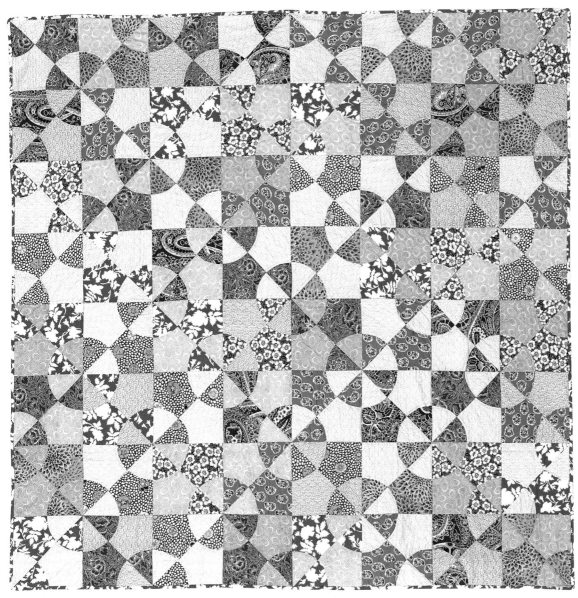

For years I've admired the strong graphic of this usually two colour design. There is something very pleasing about the rounded shapes against the straight lines. Wanting a blue and white look I picked the chalky blues in my range and soft creamy lights. When done, I saw that keeping each block in just two colours made me almost lose my circular centres. If doing the quilt again I'd put two colours in the circle sections right round so they were emphasized more.

SIZE OF QUILT
The finished quilt will measure approx. 72in x 72in (183cm x 183cm).

MATERIALS
Patchwork Fabrics:

DAHLIA BLOOMS
Pink   GP54PK: ⅝yd (60cm)
GUINEA FLOWER
Blue   GP59BL: ⅝yd (60cm)
PAISLEY JUNGLE
Blue   GP60BL: ⅝yd (60cm)

ABORIGINAL DOTS
Cream   GP71CM: 1yd (90cm)
Mint   GP71MT: ¾yd (70cm)
CLOVER
Grey   GP73GY: 1¾yds (1.6m)
Lilac   GP73LI: ¾yd (70cm)

ASHA
Blue   GP75BL: ¾yd (70cm)
SILHOUETTE ROSE
Blue   GP77BL: ¾yd (70cm)
ANENOME
Blue   GP78BL: ⅝yd (60cm)
STENCIL CARNATION
Blue   GP82BL: ¾yd (70cm)

Backing Fabric: 4¾yds (4.4m)
We suggest these fabrics for backing:
DAHLIA BLOOMS Pink, GP54PK
PAISLEY JUNGLE Blue, GP60BL

Binding:
SILHOUETTE ROSE
Blue   GP77BL: ⅝yd (60cm)

Batting:
80in × 80in (203cm × 203cm).

Quilting Thread:
Toning machine quilting thread and ivory
hand quilting thread.

Templates:

Q   R

PATCH SHAPES

The blocks for this quilt are pieced using 2
patch shapes (Templates Q and R) which are
pieced to form 2 triangles, the fabrics are in
opposite positions in each triangle. The blocks
are then straight set into rows so that the
triangle tips come together to form circles at
the junctions.

CUTTING OUT

Template Q: Cut 6½in (16.5cm) strips across
the width of the fabric. Each strip will give
you 6 patches per full width. Cut 28 in
GP73GY, 14 in GP71CM, 11 in GP71MT,
GP73LI, GP75BL, 10 in GP77BL, GP82BL, 9 in
GP59BL, 8 in GP54PK, GP60BL and GP78BL.

Template R: Cut 5½in (14cm) strips across
the width of the fabric. Each strip will give
you 14 patches per full width. Refer to the
cutting diagram and cut 56 in GP73GY, 28 in
GP71CM, 22 in GP71MT, GP73LI, GP75BL,
20 in GP77BL, GP82BL, 18 in GP59BL, 16 in
GP54PK, GP60BL and GP78BL. Cutting in this
way will ensure that each shape has one
edge cut on either the horizontal or vertical
straight grain of the fabric. These straight
grain edges should be used on the outer
edges of the blocks. Keep the shapes in pairs

as indicated by the cutting diagram, use 1 pair
for piecing each triangle (half block).

Binding: Cut 8 strips 2½in (6.5cm) wide
across the width of the fabric in GP77BL.

Backing: Cut 2 pieces 40in × 80in (101.5cm
× 203cm) in backing fabric.

MAKING THE BLOCKS

Use a ¼in (6mm) seam allowance
throughout. Each block is pieced in 2
triangular halves. In each block 2 fabrics are
used, in opposite positions in each half of the
block. Refer to the quilt assembly diagram for
fabric combinations. Take a template Q shape
and 2 template R shapes. Ensuring that the
straight grain of the fabric will be on the
outer edge of the finished block, join the
shapes as shown in block assembly diagram a.
Match the diamond markers and edges
carefully, and use plenty of pins to ease the
shapes together. You can make tiny clips in
the curved edge of the template Q shape to
make matching easier if necessary. Make 2
opposite triangles, then join the triangles as
shown in diagram b. The finished block is
shown in diagram c. Make 64 blocks.

Cutting Diagram

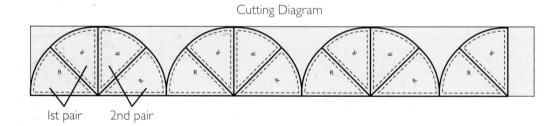

1st pair   2nd pair

Block Assembly Diagrams

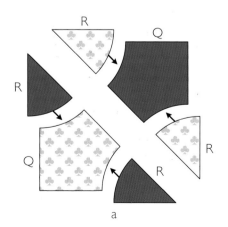

a   b   c

MAKING THE QUILT
Arrange the blocks into 8 rows as shown in the quilt assembly diagram. Join the blocks into rows, then join the rows to form the quilt.

FINISHING THE QUILT
Press the quilt top. Seam the backing pieces using a ¼in (6mm) seam allowance to form a piece approx. 80in × 80in (203cm × 203cm). Layer the quilt top, batting and backing and baste together (see page 138). Using toning machine quilting thread, stitch in the ditch around all the blocks. Then hand quilt ¼in (6mm) inside the circles at the block junctions. Trim the quilt edges and attach the binding (see page 139).

Quilt Assembly Diagram

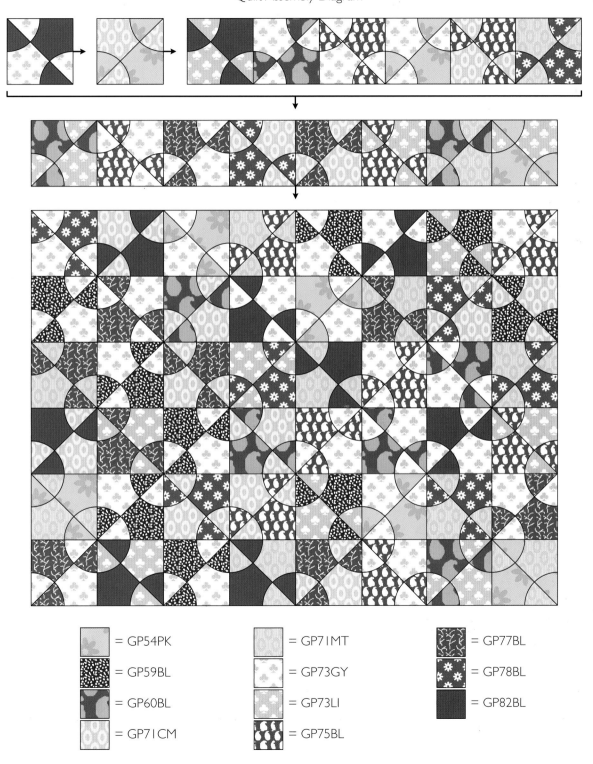

= GP54PK

= GP59BL

= GP60BL

= GP71CM

= GP71MT

= GP73GY

= GP73LI

= GP75BL

= GP77BL

= GP78BL

= GP82BL

Tulips Quilt ★★★

PAULINE SMITH

A simple pieced background in rich blues, purples and greens spills into the border. Stylized vases of tulips in jewel colours are appliquéd to the centre to complete the quilt.

SIZE OF QUILT
The finished quilt will measure approx.
49½in x 61½in (126cm x 156cm).

MATERIALS
Patchwork, Appliqué and Border Fabrics:
DAHLIA BLOOMS
Fig   GP54FI: ¼yd (25cm)

BEKAH
Magenta   GP69MG: ¼yd (25cm)
SPOT
Periwinkle   GP70PE: ½yd (45cm)
PERSIMMON
Blue   GP74BL: ⅝yd (60cm)
FLOWER DOT
Cobalt   GP87CB: ¾yd (70cm)

ASIAN CIRCLES
Dark   GP89DK: ½yd (45cm)
Green   GP89GN: 1yd (90cm)
CABBAGE PATCH
Purple   GP94PU: ¼yd (25cm)
SHOT COTTON
Jade   SC41: ⅜yd (35cm)
Viridian   SC55: ¼yd (25cm)

HAZE STRIPE
Fuchsia   S4465: ¼yd (25cm)
WOVEN MULTI STRIPE
Fuchsia   WMSFU: ¼yd (25cm)

Backing Fabric: 3½yds (3.2m)
We suggest these fabrics for backing:
ASIAN CIRCLES Dark, GP89DK
CABBAGE PATCH Purple, GP94PU
HAZE STRIPE Fuchsia, S4465

Binding:
WOVEN MULTI STRIPE
Fuchsia   WMSFU: ½yd (45cm)

Batting:
57in × 69in (145cm × 175cm).

You Will Also Need:
Adhesive web for appliqué.
Toning machine embroidery thread.

Quilting Thread:
Toning hand quilting threads.

PATCH SHAPES
The background of this pretty quilt is pieced
from a selection of rectangles, cut to size.
These are pieced into 3 columns, then joined
to form the quilt centre. Appliqué is then
added to the background. Templates are
provided for the tulips which are machine
appliquéd using adhesive web (choose the
type that requires sewing) and leaf shapes
which are hand appliquéd. The stems, vases
and embellishments are also hand appliquéd
and are cut to size. The quilt is finished with a
border pieced of strips cut to size.

CUTTING OUT
We recommend drawing out the rectangles
onto the fabric before cutting for the best fit
and to prevent waste.
Column 1:
Rectangle 1: Cut 19½in × 17½in (49.5cm ×
44.5cm) in GP89GN.
Rectangle 2: Cut 23½in × 17½in (59.75cm ×
44.5cm) in GP87CB.
Rectangle 3: Cut 10in × 17½in (25.5cm ×
44.5cm) in GP89DK.
Column 2:
Rectangle 4: Cut 27in × 6in (68.5cm ×
15.25cm) in SC41.
Rectangle 5: Cut 2in × 6in (5cm × 15.25cm)
in WMSFU.
Rectangle 6: Cut 1¾in × 6in (4.5cm ×
15.25cm) in SC41.
Rectangle 7: Cut 1½in × 6in (3.75cm ×
15.25cm) in WMSFU.

Rectangle 8: Cut 1in × 6in (2.5cm ×
15.25cm) in GP70PE.
Rectangle 9: Cut 1¼in × 6in (3.25cm ×
15.25cm) in SC41.
Rectangle 10: Cut 3½in × 6in (9cm ×
15.25cm) in WMSFU.
Rectangle 11: Cut 17½in × 6in (44.5cm ×
15.25cm) in SC41.
Column 3:
Rectangle 12: Cut 33¼in × 12in (84.5cm ×
30.5cm) in GP89GN.
Rectangle 13: Cut 8¼in × 6in (21cm ×
15.25cm) in SC41.
Rectangle 14: Cut 25½in × 6in (64.75cm ×
15.25cm) in SC55.
Rectangle 15: Cut 13¾ in × 17½in (35cm ×
44.5cm) in GP87CB.
Rectangle 16: Cut 6in × 17½in (15.25cm ×
44.5cm) in GP89DK.

Left Side Border: Cut 1 strip 5½in × 40in
(14cm × 101.5cm) in GP74BL and 1 strip
5½in × 12½in (14cm × 31.75cm) in GP70PE.
Top Border: Cut 1 strip 5½in × 28in (14cm
× 71cm) in GP70PE and 1 strip 5½in ×
17½in (14cm × 44.5cm) in GP89GN.
Right Side Border: Cut 1 strip 5½in × 21½in
(14cm × 54.5cm) in GP89GN and 1 strip
5½in × 36in (14cm × 91.5cm) in GP74BL.
Bottom Border: Cut 1 strip 5½in × 15½in
(14cm × 39.5cm) in GP70PE and 1 strip
5½in × 35in (14cm × 89cm) in GP74BL.

Appliqué Shapes:
Top Left Vase: Cut 1 rectangle 4in × 8in
(10.25cm × 20.25cm) in GP70PE and 1
embellishment strip 1¼in × 8in (3.25cm ×
20.25cm) in S4465 with the stripe direction
vertical.
Bottom Left Vase: Cut 1 rectangle 9½in ×
5¾in (24.25cm × 14.5cm) in GP94PU and 1
embellishment strip 1½in × 5¾in (3.75cm ×
14.5cm) in S4465 with the stripe direction
vertical.
Top Right Vase: Cut 1 rectangle 9½in × 6½in
(24.25cm × 16.5cm) in GP89DK and 1
embellishment strip 1½in × 6½in (3.75cm ×
16.5cm) in GP70PE.
Bottom Right Vase: Cut 1 rectangle × 5½in ×
8¾in (14cm × 22.25cm) in S4465 with the
stripe direction vertical and 1 embellishment
strip 1½in × 8¾in (3.75cm × 22.25cm) in
GP70PE.
Stems: These are hand appliquéd. Cut 1in
(2.5cm) wide bias strips. Cut 5 in SC55, 4 in
WMSFU 2 in GP69MG and GP70PE. The
stems vary from 4in to 12in (10cm to
30.5cm) in length, refer to the photograph
and the appliqué and border diagram for

length and placement and remember to
allow a little extra length to tuck into the
vase tops and sit behind the tulips.
Leaves: These are hand appliquéd. the
appliqué shapes on page 130 do not include
a seam allowance. Make a selection of card
or plastic leaf shapes. Draw round the shapes
onto the reverse of the fabrics, add a seam
allowance of about ¼in (6mm) all around
and cut the leaves out. Cut 8 in SC55, 3 in
GP70PE, 2 in WMSFU and 1 in GP69MG.
Tulip Flowers: These are machine appliquéd
using adhesive web, use the type that
requires sewing. Make a card or plastic tulip
template. Draw around the tulip template 13
times, flipping the template over to vary the
shape, onto the paper side of your adhesive
web, leaving a ¼in (6mm) gap between the
shapes. Roughly cut out the tulips about ⅛in
(3mm) outside your drawn line. Bond the
tulips to the REVERSE of the fabrics referring
to the photograph to see the areas of the
fabric used for each flower. Bond 7 in GP54FI
and 6 in GP69MG.

Binding: Cut 6 strips 2½in (6.5cm) wide ×
width of fabric in WMSFU.

Backing: Cut 1 piece 40in × 57in (101.5cm ×
145cm) and 1 piece 30in × 57in (76cm ×
145cm) in backing fabric.

MAKING THE QUILT CENTRE
Use a ¼in (6mm) seam allowance
throughout. Referring to the quilt centre
assembly diagram for fabric placement, piece
3 columns as shown in the quilt centre
assembly diagram. Join the columns to form
the quilt centre.

APPLIQUÉ AND BORDER
Refer to the Patchwork Know How Appliqué
section from page 137 for appliqué
techniques and to the appliqué and border
assembly diagram and photographs for
appliqué positioning and fabrics.

Press a ¼in (6mm) seam allowance along the
long sides of each embellishment strip and
hand appliqué into place onto the vases.
Press a ¼in (6mm) seam allowance around
each vase shape. Apply the vases to the quilt
centre, leaving the top edge unstitched for
now so that the stems can be tucked into the
tops of the vases. Press a ¼in (6mm)
seam allowance along the long sides of each
stem and pin into position on the quilt
centre. Add the leaves using the finger
pressing method and stitch into place tucking

the tips under the stems. Stitch the stems into place, leaving the tops and bottoms raw as these will be covered by the vase and tulip shapes and then finish the top edges of the vases.

Cut out the bonded tulip shapes with very sharp scissors on the drawn line. Remove the backing papers by scoring the paper in the middle of the shape and peeling the paper from the centre out, this prevents damage to the edges. Arrange the tulips as shown in the appliqué and border assembly diagram, covering the tops of the stems. Once all the shapes are correctly positioned bond into place. Stitch using a toning machine embroidery thread and a blanket or zigzag stitch. The stitching should sit mostly on the bonded shape.

Piece the borders then add them to the quilt centre in the order shown in the appliqué and border assembly diagram.

Quilt Centre Assembly Diagram

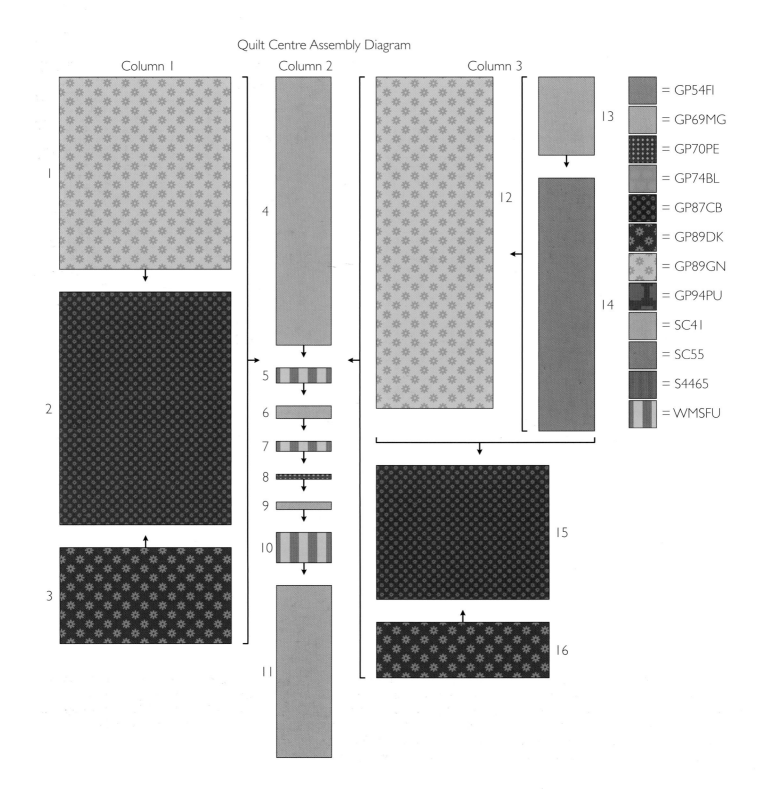

Appliqué and Border Diagram

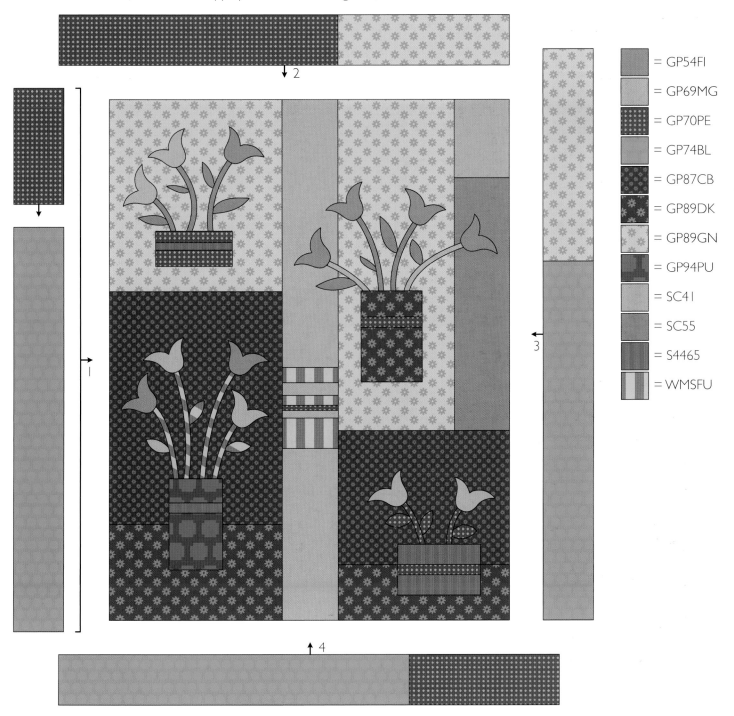

= GP54FI
= GP69MG
= GP70PE
= GP74BL
= GP87CB
= GP89DK
= GP89GN
= GP94PU
= SC41
= SC55
= S4465
= WMSFU

FINISHING THE QUILT

Press the quilt top. Seam the backing pieces using a ¼in (6mm) seam allowance to form a piece approx. 57in x 69in (145cm x 175cm). Layer the quilt top, batting and backing and baste together (see page 138). Using toning hand quilting threads echo quilt around the appliqué shapes offset by about ¼in (6mm). Then pick out shapes in the floral fabrics and quilt circles and floral shapes throughout the quilt centre. In the Shot Cotton areas quilt vertical and horizontal lines spaced randomly, avoiding the appliquéd shapes. The border is quilted with 2 parallel lines, spaced at 1½in and 3in (3.75cm and 7.5cm) from the inner seam. (Trim the quilt edges and attach the binding (see page 139).

Ice Cream Quilt ★★

KAFFE FASSETT

Radiating squares is a layout I always find compelling when I see it in old carpets and other textiles. I also love soft–pastel old quilts, so I combined the two and did this soft quilt with a dynamic profile. Any pastel fabrics could be used such as my new pastel colourways of Spot or Tulip Mania.

SIZE OF QUILT
The finished quilt will measure approx.
77½in x 81½in (197cm x 207cm).

MATERIALS
Patchwork Fabrics:
LOTUS LEAF
Pastel   GP29PT: 1yd (90cm)
KIMONO
Lavender/Blue   GP33LB: 1⅛yds (1m)
GUINEA FLOWER
Mauve   GP59MV: ½yd (45cm)

ABORIGINAL DOTS
Cream   GP71CM: ⅞yd (80cm)
Sweet Pea   GP71SW: ¾yd (70cm)
LICHEN
Celadon   GP76CD: ¾yd (70cm)
STENCIL
Cream   GP79CM: ½yd (45cm)
Opal   GP79OP: ¼yd (25cm)
TULIP
White   PJ14WH: ¾yd (70cm)
LILAC ROSE
Pink   PJ17PK: ⅜yd (35cm)

IVY
Grey   PJ19GY: 1yd (90cm)
Pink   PJ19PK: ⅜yd (35cm)

Backing Fabric: 6yds (5.5m)
We suggest these fabrics for backing:
GUINEA FLOWER Mauve, GP59MV
KIMONO Lavender/Blue, GP33LB
LILAC ROSE Pink, PJ17PK

Binding:
IVY

Pink   PJ19PK: ¾yd (70cm)

Batting:
85½in × 89½in (217cm × 227.5cm).

Quilting Thread:
Toning hand quilting threads.

PATCH SHAPES
This quilt is constructed around a rectangular centre panel (cut to size). Strips are then added, 'log cabin' style around the centre. Each 'round' of logs are cut to size in the same width and fabric. A total of 20 'rounds' of logs are added to complete the quilt.

CUTTING OUT
Centre Panel: Cut 1 rectangle 5in × 9in (12.75cm × 22.75cm) in GP76CD. The following table shows the 'round' number, fabric code, width of logs, the number of strips across the width of the

fabric needed for each 'round of logs' (join fabric strips as necessary). It also shows the length of each log. All measurements INCLUDE a ¼in (6mm) seam allowance. The final column shows the size that your quilt should be after adding each 'round' of logs, also including the seam allowance. It is not critical for your quilt to be perfectly sized, but it does help to keep your patchwork in true as working with narrow strips can be a little tricky.

Binding: Cut 9 strips 2½in (6.5cm) wide across the width of the fabric in PJ19PK.

Backing: Cut 2 pieces 40in × 85½in (101.5cm × 217cm), 2 pieces 40in × 10in (101.5cm × 25.5cm) and 1 piece 10in × 6in (25.5cm × 15.25cm) in backing fabric.

MAKING THE QUILT
Use a ¼in (6mm) seam allowance

throughout. Take the centre panel and add 'round 1' Log A to the bottom of the centre panel, followed by Log B on the left side, Log C is added to the top and Log D to the right side to complete round 1. This is shown in the assembly diagram – round 1, Round 2 is shown in the round 2 diagram. Press carefully after adding each log. In every 'round' the logs are added in the same sequence. Add all 20 'rounds' of logs as shown in the quilt assembly diagram.

FINISHING THE QUILT
Press the quilt top. Seam the backing pieces using a ¼in (6mm) seam allowance to form a piece approx. 85½in × 89½in (217cm × 227.5cm). Layer the quilt top, batting and backing and baste together (see page 138). Hand quilt a line through the centre of each log using toning hand quilting thread. Trim the quilt edges and attach the binding (see page 139).

Round	Fabric	Log Width	# of strips	Log A	Log B	Log C	Log D	Size to raw edge
1	PJ19GY	1¾in (4.5cm)	1	5in (12.75cm)	10¼in (26cm)	6¼in (16cm)	11½in (29.25cm)	7½in × 11½in (19cm × 29.25cm)
2	PJ14WH	2in (5cm)	2	7½in (19cm)	13in (33cm)	9in (22.75cm)	14½in (36.75cm)	10½in × 14½in (26.75cm × 36.75cm)
3	GP79OP	2in (5cm)	2	10½in (26.75cm)	16in (40.75cm)	12in (30.5cm)	17½in (44.5cm)	13½in × 17½in (34.25cm × 44.5cm)
4	GP79CM	2½in (6.25cm)	2	13½in (34.25cm	19½in (49.5cm	15½in (39.5cm)	21½in (54.5cm)	17½in × 21½in (44.5cm × 54.5cm)
5	GP29PT	2in (5cm)	3	17½in (44.5cm)	23in (58.5cm)	19in (48.25cm)	24½in (62.25cm)	20½in × 24½in (52cm × 62.25cm)
6	GP71SW	1¾in (4.5cm)	3	20½in (52cm)	25¾in (65.5cm)	21¾in (55.25cm)	27in (68.5cm)	23in × 27in (58.5cm × 68.5cm)
7	GP33LB	3in (7.5cm)	3	23in (58.5cm)	29½in (75cm)	25½in (64.75cm)	32in (81.25cm)	28in × 32in (71cm × 81.25cm)
8	PJ19PK	2in (5cm)	4	28in (71cm)	23½in (85cm)	29½in (75cm)	35in (89cm)	31in × 35in (78.75cm × 89cm)
9	GP79CM	2in (5cm)	4	31in (78.75cm)	36½in (92.75cm)	32½in (82.5cm)	38in (96.5cm)	34in × 38in (86.25cm × 96.5cm)
10	GP59MV	3in (7.5cm)	4	34in (86.25cm)	40½in (103cm)	36½in (92.75cm)	43in (109.25cm)	39in × 43in (99cm × 109.25cm)
11	GP71CM	2in (5cm)	5	39in (99cm)	44½in (113cm)	40½in (103cm)	46in (116.75cm)	42in × 46in (106.75cm × 116.75cm)
12	PJ19GY	2½in (6.25cm)	5	42in (106.75cm)	48in (122cm)	44in (111.75cm)	50in (127cm)	46in × 50in (116.75cm × 127cm)
13	GP29PT	4in (10.25cm)	6	46in (116.75cm)	53½in (136cm)	49½in (125.75cm)	57in (144.75cm)	53in × 57in (134.5cm × 144.75cm)
14	PJ17PK	1½in (3.75cm)	6	53in (134.5cm)	58in (147.25cm)	54in (137.25cm)	59in (149.75cm)	55in × 59in (139.75cm × 149.75cm)
15	GP71CM	2½in (6.25cm)	6	55in (139.75cm)	61in (155cm)	57in (144.75cm)	63in (160cm)	59in × 63in (149.75cm × 160cm)
16	PJ19GY	2in (5cm)	7	59in (149.75cm)	64½in (163.75cm)	60½in (153.75cm)	66in (167.75cm)	62in × 66in (157.5cm × 167.75cm)
17	PJ14WH	2½in (6.25cm)	7	62in (157.50cm)	68in (172.75cm)	64in (162.5cm)	70in (177.75cm)	66in × 70in (167.75cm × 177.75cm)
18	GP76CD	2½in (6.25cm)	7	66in (167.75cm)	72in (183cm)	68in (172.75cm)	74in (188cm)	70in × 74in (177.75cm × 188cm)
19	GP71SW	2in (5cm)	8	70in (177.75cm)	75½in (191.75cm)	71½in (181.5cm)	77in (195.5cm)	73in × 77in (185.5cm × 195.5cm)
20	GP33LB	3in (7.5cm)	8	73in (185.5cm)	79½in (202cm)	75½in (191.75cm)	82in (208.25cm)	78in × 82in (198cm × 208.25cm)

Quilt Assembly Diagram

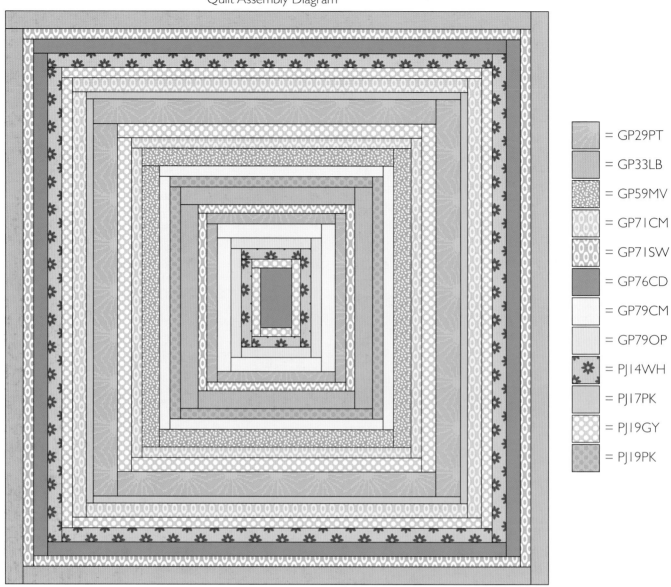

= GP29PT
= GP33LB
= GP59MV
= GP71CM
= GP71SW
= GP76CD
= GP79CM
= GP79OP
= PJ14WH
= PJ17PK
= PJ19GY
= PJ19PK

Assembly Diagram – Round 1

Assembly Diagram – Round 2

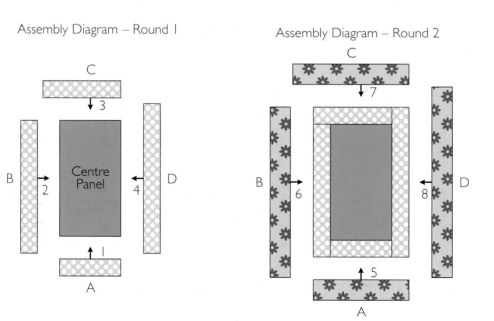

Pastel Italian Tiles Quilt ★★

KAFFE FASSETT

Because I knew the benches and the many architectural details at Portmeirion were painted a light turquoise I used that colour for the sashings in this quilt. It fits right in — the silvery pastel prints set off perfectly by the turquoise.

SIZE OF QUILT
The finished quilt will measure approx.
83in x 83in (211cm x 211cm).

MATERIALS
Patchwork and Border Fabrics:
ROMAN GLASS
Pink   GP01PK: ⅜yd (35cm)

KIMONO
Lavender/Blue   GP33LB: ⅜yd (35cm)
Pink/Orange   GP33PO: ⅜yd (35cm)
FLOATING FLOWERS
Pink   GP56PK: ⅜yd (35cm)
Pastel   GP56PT: ⅜yd (35cm)
PAPER FANS
Cream   GP57CM: ⅜yd (35cm)

SILHOUETTE ROSE
Duck Egg   GP77DE: ⅜yd (35cm)
ANEMONE
Pink   GP78PK: ⅜yd (35cm)
WINDING FLORAL
Pastel   GP85PT: ⅜yd (35cm)
ASIAN CIRCLES
Pink   GP89PK: ⅜yd (35cm)

TALL HOLLYHOCKS
Opal   PJ16OP: 3½yds (3.2m)
LILAC ROSE
Pink   PJ17PK: ⅜yd (35cm)
SHOT COTTON
Jade   SC41: 2¼yds (2.1m)

Backing Fabric: 6½yds (6m)
We suggest these fabrics for backing:
WOVEN MULTI STRIPE Red, WMSRD or
Teal, WMSTE

Binding:
MILLEFIORE
Pastel   GP92PT: ¾yd (70cm)
Batting:
91in x 91in (231cm x 231cm)

Quilting Thread:
Toning machine quilting thread.

Templates:

N   O   P

Large Square

PATCH SHAPES
The 'tiles' blocks (finish to 10in (24.5cm) are pieced using a triangle patch shape (Template N), a lozenge patch shape (Template O) and a square patch shape (Template P). The blocks are alternated with large squares, cut to size, then surrounded with a simple border to complete the quilt.

CUTTING OUT
Border: Cut 9 strips 2in (5cm) wide across the width of the fabric in SC41. Join as necessary and cut 2 strips 2in x 80½in (5cm x 204.5cm) for the quilt sides and 2 strips 2in x 83½in (5cm x 212cm) for the quilt top and bottom.
Template O: Cut 2in (5cm) strips across the width of the fabric. Each strip will give you 5 patches per full width. Cut 128 in SC41.
Template N: Cut 9⅛in (23.25cm) strips across the width of the fabric. Each strip will give you 16 triangles per full width. Cut 9⅛in (23.25cm) squares, cut each square twice diagonally to form 4 triangles using the template as a guide, this will ensure that the long side of the triangle will not have a bias edge. Note: do not move the patches until both the diagonals have been cut. Cut 12 triangles in GP01PK, GP33LB, GP56PK, GP56PT, GP57CM, GP77DE, GP78PK, GP85PT, GP89PK, PJ17PK and 8 in GP33PO. Reserve leftover fabric for template P.
Template P: Using the leftover fabric from template N, cut 2in (5cm) squares. Cut 3 in GP01PK, GP33LB, GP56PK, GP56PT, GP57CM, GP77DE, GP78PK, GP85PT, GP89PK, PJ17PK and 2 in GP33PO.
Large Squares: Cut 10½in (26.75cm) strips across the width of the fabric. Each strip will give you 3 patches per full width. Cut 10½in (26.75cm) squares. Cut 32 in PJ16OP.

Binding: Cut 9 strips 2½in (6.5cm) wide across the width of the fabric in GP92PT.

Backing: Cut 2 pieces 40in x 91in (101.5cm x 231cm), 2 pieces 40in x 12in (101.5cm x 30.5cm) and 1 piece 12in x 12in (30.5cm x 30.5cm) in backing fabric.

MAKING THE BLOCKS
Use a ¼in (6mm) seam allowance throughout. Each 'tiles' block is made using 4 template N triangles, 1 template P square in the same fabric and 4 template O lozenges. Piece a total of 32 blocks following block assembly diagrams a and b. The finished block is shown in diagram c.

MAKING THE QUILT
Lay out the blocks, alternating them with the large squares as shown in the quilt assembly diagram. Join into 8 rows of 8 blocks. Join the rows to complete the quilt centre. Add the side borders to the quilt centre, then the top and bottom borders to complete the quilt.

FINISHING THE QUILT
Press the quilt top. Seam the backing pieces using a ¼in (6mm) seam allowance to form a piece approx. 91in x 91in (231cm x 231cm). Layer the quilt top, batting and backing and baste together (see page 138). Machine quilt using toning quilting thread, stitch in the ditch in the 'tiles' blocks and meander quilt the large squares following the floral designs in the fabric. Trim the quilt edges and attach the binding (see page 139).

Block Assembly Diagrams

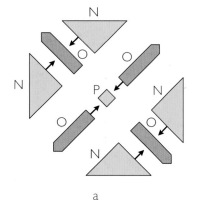

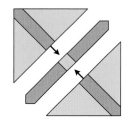

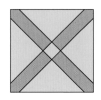

a   b   c

Quilt Assembly Diagram

Large Square

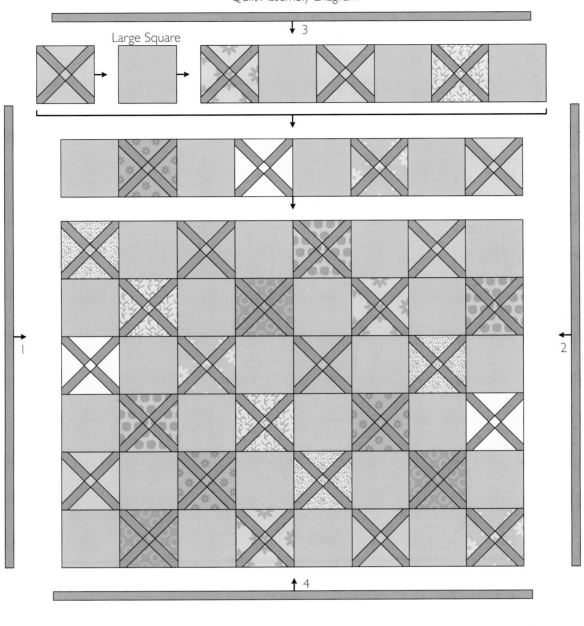

	= GP01PK		= GP56PK		= GP77DE		= GP89PK
	= GP33LB		= GP56PT		= GP78PK		= PJ16OP
	= GP33PO		= GP57CM		= GP85PT		= PJ17PK
							= SC41

Gold Italian Tiles Quilt ★★

Kaffe Fassett

The high golden yellow of this colour scheme lights me up – like a field of buttercups on a summer day. Such a good way to show upscale florals.

SIZE OF QUILT
The finished quilt will measure approx.
91in x 91in (231cm x 231cm).

MATERIALS
Patchwork and Border Fabrics:

LOTUS LEAF
Yellow   GP29YE: ⅜yd (35cm)
DAHLIA BLOOMS
Vintage   GP54VN: 1⅝yds (1.5m)
       incl. borders
GUINEA FLOWER
Mauve   GP59MV: ⅜yd (35cm)
PAISLEY JUNGLE
Tangerine   GP60TN: ⅜yd (35cm)
SPOT
Fuchsia   GP70FU: ⅜yd (35cm)
Yellow   GP70YE: ⅜yd (35cm)
PERSIMMON
Orange   GP74OR: ⅜yd (35cm)
ASHA
Yellow   GP75YE: ⅞yd (80cm)
       incl. borders
SILHOUETTE ROSE
Tortoiseshell   GP77TS: ⅜yd (35cm)
STENCIL
Gold   GP79GD: 4yds (3.7m)
       incl. extra fabric for
       fussy cutting.

TURKISH DELIGHT
Gold   GP81GD: ⅜yd (35cm)
MILLEFIORE
Brown   GP92BR: ⅜yd (35cm)
GRANDIOSE
Ochre   PJ13OC: ⅜yd (35cm)
TULIP
Yellow   PJ14YE: ⅜yd (35cm)
BEGONIA LEAVES
Gold   PJ18GD: ⅜yd (35cm)
SHOT COTTON
Rosy   SC32: ⅜yd (35cm)
Butter   SC64: ⅜yd (35cm)
Backing Fabric: 7¾yds (7.1m)

We suggest these fabrics for backing:
TURKISH DELIGHT Gold, GP81GD
MILLEFIORE Brown, GP92BR
GRANDIOSE Ochre, PJ13OC

Binding:
SPOT
Yellow   GP70YE: ¾yd (70cm)

Batting:
99in x 99in (251.5cm x 251.5cm)

Quilting Thread:
Toning machine quilting thread.

Templates:
See Pastel Italian Tiles Quilt instructions.

PATCH SHAPES
See Pastel Italian Tiles Quilt instructions.
Note: In this version of the quilt, the large
squares are 'fussy cut' and it also has an
additional outer border.

CUTTING OUT
Inner Border: Cut 9 strips 2in (5cm) wide
across the width of the fabric in GP75YE. Join
as necessary and cut 2 strips 2in x 80½in
(5cm x 204.5cm) for the quilt sides and 2
strips 2in x 83½in (5cm x 212cm) for the
quilt top and bottom.
Outer Border: Cut 9 strips 4½in (11.5cm)
wide across the width of the fabric in
GP54VN. Join as necessary and cut 2 strips
4½in x 83½in (11.5cm x 212cm) for the quilt
sides and 2 strips 4½in x 91½in (11.5cm x
232.5cm) for the quilt top and bottom.
Template N: Cut 9⅛in (23.25cm) strips
across the width of the fabric. Each strip will
give you 16 triangles per full width. Cut 9⅛in
(23.25cm) squares, cut each square twice
diagonally to form 4 triangles using the
template as a guide, this will ensure that the
long side of the triangle will not have a bias

edge. Note: do not move the patches until
both the diagonals have been cut. Cut 16
triangles in GP29YE, GP54VN, GP60TN,
GP74OR, GP81GD, PJ13OC, PJ14YE and
PJ18GD. Reserve leftover fabric for template P.
Template P: Using the leftover fabric from
template N, cut 2in (5cm) squares. Cut 4 in
GP29YE, GP54VN, GP60TN, GP74OR,
GP81GD, PJ13OC, PJ14YE and PJ18GD.
Template O: Cut 2in (5cm) strips across the
width of the fabric. Each strip will give you 5
patches per full width. Cut 16 in GP59MV,
GP70FU, GP70YE, GP75YE, GP77TS,
GP92BR, SC32 and SC64.
Large Squares: Cut 10½in (26.75cm) squares
centred in the motifs as shown in the
photograph. Cut 32 in GP79GD.

Binding: Cut 9 strips 2½in (6.5cm) wide
across the width of the fabric in GP70YE.

Backing: Cut 2 pieces 40in x 99in (101.5cm
x 251.5cm), 2 pieces 40in x 20in (101.5cm x
51cm) and 1 piece 20in x 20in (51cm x
51cm) in backing fabric.

MAKING THE BLOCKS
See Pastel Italian Tiles Quilt instructions.

MAKING THE QUILT
See Pastel Italian Tiles Quilt instructions.
Note: Add the additional outer border in the
same way as the inner border.

FINISHING THE QUILT
Press the quilt top. Seam the backing pieces
using a ¼in (6mm) seam allowance to form a
piece approx. 99in x 99in (251.5cm x
251.5cm). Layer the quilt top, batting and
backing and baste together (see page 138).
Machine quilt using toning quilting thread,
stitch in the ditch in the 'tiles' blocks and
meander quilt the large squares following the
floral designs in the fabric. Trim the quilt
edges and attach the binding (see page 139).

Quilt Assembly Diagram

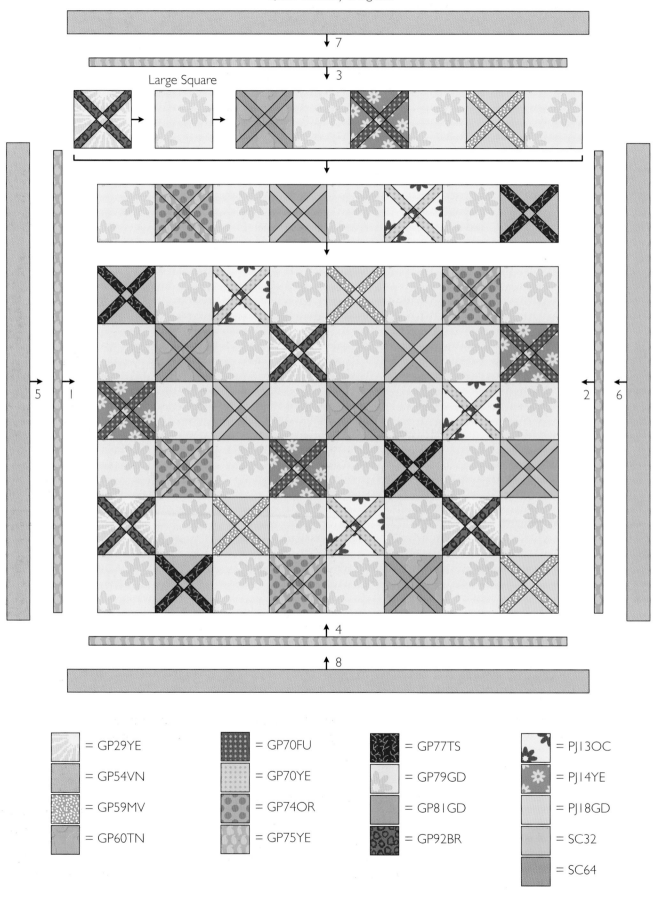

Large Square

	= GP29YE		= GP70FU		= GP77TS		= PJ13OC
	= GP54VN		= GP70YE		= GP79GD		= PJ14YE
	= GP59MV		= GP74OR		= GP81GD		= PJ18GD
	= GP60TN		= GP75YE		= GP92BR		= SC32
							= SC64

Spring Log Cabin Quilt ★★

LIZA PRIOR LUCY

I had never heard about Portmeirion until Kaffe and Pauline told me about it. In describing where the shoot for this book was to take place, they emphasized the colours of the buildings. I decided that I would do my favourite quilt pattern in the pinks and yellows of that magical place.

SIZE OF QUILT
The finished quilt will measure approx.
80in x 80in (203cm x 203cm).

MATERIALS
This fabric list is a guide, don't worry about

substituting other fabrics if some are not available. The only key fabrics are the Diagonal Stripes which form the final 'round' of logs for each block and the Big Blooms fabric which is fussy cut for the block centres.
Patchwork Fabrics:

DIAGONAL STRIPES
Pink   GP90PK: 1½yds (1.4m)
Yellow   GP90YE: 1½yds (1.4m)
BIG BLOOMS
Pink   GP91PK: 1yd (90cm)*
*Extra fabric allowed for fussy cutting.

Buy ⅜yd (35cm) of each of the following fabrics.

Light Patchwork Fabrics:

PAPERWEIGHT Lime	GP20LM
PAPER FANS Yellow	GP57YE
SPOT Pink	GP70PK
DAISY Cream	GP80CM
CLOUDS Duck Egg	GP86DE
STAR FLOWER Pastel	GP88PT
ASIAN CIRCLES Yellow	GP89YE
LAKE BLOSSOMS Yellow	GP93YE

Dark Patchwork Fabrics:

ZINNIA Pink	GP31PK
CLOISONNE Magenta	GP46MG
FLOWER BASKET Magenta	GP48MG
FLOATING FLOWERS Scarlet	
	GP56SC
GUINEA FLOWER Apricot	GP59AP
SPOT Fuchsia	GP70FU
LICHEN Rust	GP76RU
ASIAN CIRCLES Tomato	GP89TM

Backing Fabric: 6yds (5.5m)
We suggest these fabrics for backing:
ZINNIA Pink, GP31PK
STAR FLOWER Pastel, GP88PT
LAKE BLOSSOMS Yellow, GP93YE

Binding:
ABORIGINAL DOTS
Lime   GP71LM: ¾yd (70cm)

Batting:
88in x 88in (223.5cm x 223.5cm).

Quilting Thread:
Toning machine quilting threads.

PATCH SHAPES
Log cabin blocks are pieced from logs (cut to size) around a fussy cut square (Template G). The final 'round' of logs is cut from Diagonal Stripe fabric and the direction of the stripes is visually important. The blocks are then arranged in the traditional 'Straight Furrow' layout.

Templates:

G

CUTTING OUT
This quilt is scrappy so it isn't necessary to place each fabric as in the original. Just keep the light fabrics on one side of the block and the darks on the other. The key fabrics are the fussy cut centres (template G) and the final 'round' of logs where the stripe direction is important. There are 2 types of block, the only difference between them is the stripe direction in the final 'round' of logs.

Template G: Centring on the blooms fussy cut 25 x 4½in (11.5cm) squares in GP91PK.

Outside Logs: Cut 2in (5cm) strips down the length of the fabric, parallel to the selvedge and make sure that each pair of logs has the stripes slanting in the same direction. Note: You will need 13 sets of logs with the stripes slanting //// for Block 1 and 12 sets with the stripes slanting \\\\ for Block 2. Refer to the block diagrams for help. When cutting discard any strips that have 'V' points where the stripes change direction.

Cut 25 Pairs of Logs in GP90PK: Logs 13 and 14, 13½in (34.25cm) and 15in (38cm), see note above regarding stripe direction.

Cut 25 Pairs of Logs in GP90YE: Logs 15 and 16, 15in (38cm) and 16½in (42cm), see note above regarding stripe direction.

Light and Dark Fabrics: cut 2in (5cm) strips across the width of the fabric. Refer to the Log Cabin diagram and cut the fabric in pairs of logs, so that the same fabric is used in each 'L' on either side of the centre.

Cut 25 pairs of Dark Logs:
Logs 1 and 2, 4½in (11.5cm) and 6in (15.25cm) long
Logs 5 and 6, 7½in (19cm) and 9in (23cm) long
Logs 9 and 10, 10½in (26.75cm) and 12in (30.5cm)

Cut 25 pairs of Light Logs:
Logs 3 and 4, 6in (15.25cm) and 7½in (19cm) long
Logs 7 and 8, 9in (23cm) and 10½in (26.75cm) long
Logs 11 and 12, 12in (30.5cm) and 13½in (34.25cm)

Binding: Cut 9 strips 2½in (6.5cm) wide across the width of the fabric in GP71LM.

Backing: Cut 2 pieces 40in x 88in (101.5cm

Block Diagrams

Block 1

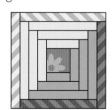

Block 2

Log Cabin Block

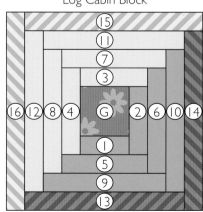

x 223.5cm), 2 pieces 40in x 9in (101.5cm x 22.75cm) and 1 piece 9in x 9in (22.75cm x 22.75cm) in backing fabric. Note: For a quirky look to the backing you could cut the 9in (22.75cm) square from a different fabric and piece the backing with the contrasting square in the centre.

MAKING THE BLOCKS
Use a ¼in (6mm) seam allowance throughout. Piece the log cabin blocks, the 'logs' are added in numerical order to the block centre (template G squares) as shown

in the log cabin diagram, remember to use the same fabric in each 'L' on either side of the centre. Make 13 of Block 1 and 12 of Block 2. The only difference between the blocks is the stripe direction of the logs in the final 'round'.

MAKING THE QUILT
Arrange the blocks as shown in the quilt assembly diagram, the block types (1 and 2) alternate throughout the quilt to produce the interesting chevron stripe effect at the block intersections.

Join the blocks into 5 rows of 5 blocks, join the rows to complete the quilt.

FINISHING THE QUILT
Press the quilt top. Seam the backing pieces using a ¼in (6mm) seam allowance to form a piece approx. 88in x 88in (223.5cm x 223.5cm). Layer the quilt top, batting and backing and baste together (see page 138). Meander quilt using yellow toning thread for the light sections and pink/orange thread for the dark sections. Trim the quilt edges and attach the binding (see page 139).

Quilt Assembly Diagaram

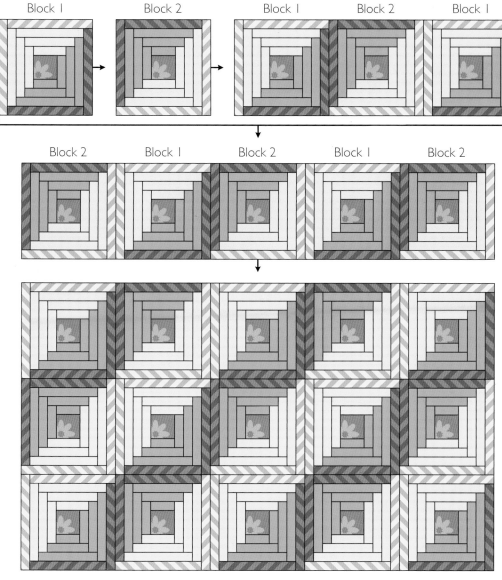

| Block 1 | Block 2 | Block 1 | Block 2 | Block 1 |

| Block 2 | Block 1 | Block 2 | Block 1 | Block 2 |

= GP90PK
= GP90YE
= GP91PK
= Light Fabrics
= Dark Fabrics

Autumn Log Cabin Quilt ★★

Liza Prior Lucy

I enjoyed making the yellow and pink version so much that I decided to do one that would be a bit a little less feminine. I still wanted it to fit into the colours of Portmeirion so this time I went for the colours of the sea and rocks.

SIZE OF QUILT
The finished quilt will measure approx.
96in x 96in (244cm x 244cm).

MATERIALS
This fabric list is a guide, don't worry about substituting other fabrics if some are not available. The only key fabric is the Big Blooms fabric which is fussy cut for the block centres.

Patchwork Fabrics:
BIG BLOOMS

Turquoise	GP91TQ: 1¼yd (1.15m)*

*Extra fabric allowed for fussy cutting.

Buy ⅝yd (60cm) of each of the following fabrics.

Light Patchwork Fabrics:
PAPERWEIGHT Lime	GP20LM
PAPERWEIGHT Sludge	GP20SL
DAHLIA BLOOMS Succulent	GP54SC
FLOATING FLOWERS Green	GP56GN
PAPER FANS Vintage	GP57VN
GUINEA FLOWER Green	GP59GN
DANCING LEAVES Jade	GP83JA
WINDING FLORAL Jade	GP85JA
ASIAN CIRCLES Green	GP89GN
MILLEFIORE Green	GP92GN

Dark Patchwork Fabrics:
ROMAN GLASS Byzantine	GP01BY
PAPERWEIGHT Teal	GP20TE
LOTUS LEAF Umber	GP29UM
ZINNIA Antique	GP31AN
DAHLIA BLOOMS Fig	GP54FI
PAISLEY JUNGLE Moss	GP60MS
PAISLEY JUNGLE Purple	GP60PU
DANCING LEAVES Moss	GP83MS
CLOUDS Charcoal	GP86CC
MILLEFIORE Blue	GP92BL

Backing Fabric: 9¼yds (8.5m)
We suggest these fabrics for backing:
ZINNIA Aqua, GP31AQ
PAPERWEIGHT Teal, GP20TE
PAISLEY JUNGLE Moss, GP60MS

Binding:
ABORIGINAL DOTS
Chocolate	GP71CL: ⅞yd (80cm)

Batting:
104in x 104in (264cm x 264cm).

Quilting Thread:
Medium taupe machine quilting threads.

PATCH SHAPES
Log cabin blocks are pieced from logs (cut to size) around a fussy cut square (Template G). The blocks are then arranged in the traditional 'Barn Raising' layout.

Templates: See Spring Log Cabin Quilt

CUTTING OUT
This quilt is scrappy so it isn't necessary to place each fabric as in the original, except the block centres (template G squares). Just keep the light fabrics on one side of the block and the darks on the other.

Template G: Centring on the blooms fussy cut 36 x 4½in (11.5cm) squares in GP91TQ.

Light and Dark Fabrics: cut 2in (5cm) strips across the width of the fabric. Refer to the Log Cabin diagram and cut the fabric in pairs of logs, so that the same fabric is used in each 'L' on either side of the centre.

Cut 36 pairs of Dark Logs:
Logs 1 and 2, 4½in (11.5cm) and 6in (15.25cm) long
Logs 5 and 6, 7½in (19cm) and 9in (23cm) long
Logs 9 and 10, 10½in (26.75cm) and 12in (30.5cm) long
Logs 13 and 14, 13½in (34.25cm) and 15in (38cm) long

Cut 36 pairs of Light Logs:
Logs 3 and 4, 6in (15.25cm) and 7½in (19cm) long
Logs 7 and 8, 9in (23cm) and 10½in (26.75cm) long
Logs 11 and 12, 12in (30.5cm) and 13½in (34.25cm) long
Logs 15 and 16, 15in (38cm) and 16½in (42cm) long.

Binding: Cut 10 strips 2½in (6.5cm) wide across the width of the fabric in GP71CL.

Backing: Cut 2 pieces 40in x 104in (101.5cm x 264cm) and 1 piece 25in x 104in (63.5cm

Log Cabin Block

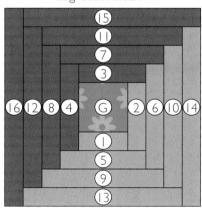

x 264cm) in backing fabric.

MAKING THE BLOCKS
Use a ¼in (6mm) seam allowance
throughout. Piece the log cabin blocks, the
'logs' are added in numerical order to the
block centre (template G squares) as shown
in the log cabin diagram, remember to use
the same fabric in each 'L' on either side of

the centre. Make 36 blocks.

MAKING THE QUILT
Arrange the blocks as shown in the quilt
assembly diagram, we recommend using a
design wall or laying the blocks out on the
floor to check the layout. Join the blocks into
6 rows of 6 blocks, join the rows to
complete the quilt.

FINISHING THE QUILT
Press the quilt top. Seam the backing pieces
using a ¼in (6mm) seam allowance to form a
piece approx. 104in x 104in (264cm x
264cm). Layer the quilt top, batting and
backing and baste together (see page 138).
Meander quilt using medium taupe machine
quilting thread. Trim the quilt edges and
attach the binding (see page 139).

Quilt Assembly Diagaram

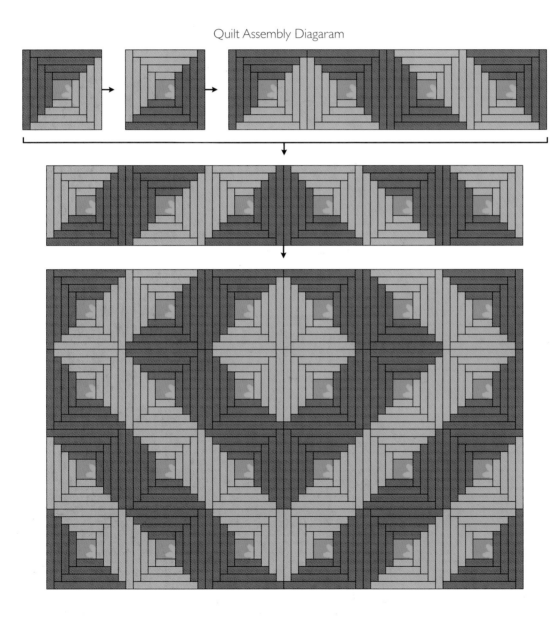

= GP91TQ

= Dark Fabrics

= Light Fabrics

Magic Carpet Quilt ★★
ROBERTA HORTON

A simple ninepatch that provides you a pathway of escape to float to places where you would rather be....

SIZE OF QUILT
The finished quilt will measure approx.
70in x 84in (178cm x 213.5cm).

MATERIALS
Patchwork Fabrics:
STAR FLOWER
Prune   GP88PR: ⅝yd (60cm)
LAKE BLOSSOMS
Green   GP93GN: ⅞yd (80cm)
CABBAGE PATCH
Magenta   GP94MG: 1⅝yd (1.5m)
Purple   GP94PU: 1yd (90cm)

Border Fabrics:
CLOUDS
Red   GP86RD: ½yd (45cm)
DIAGONAL STRIPE
Ochre   GP90OC: ½yd (45cm)
LAKE BLOSSOMS
Black   GP93BK: 1¼yds (1.15m)
WOVEN BOLD STRIPE
Fuchsia   WBSFU: ⅜yd (35cm)

Backing Fabric: 5½yds (5m)
We suggest these fabrics for backing:
BIG BLOOMS Teal, GP91TE

LAKE BLOSSOMS Black, GP93BK
LAKE BLOSSOMS Blue, GP93BL

Binding:
WOVEN BOLD STRIPE
Lavender   WBSLV: ¾yd (70cm)

Batting:
78in x 92in (198cm x 233.5cm).

Quilting Thread:
Invisible, purple, red and green machine quilting threads.

Templates:

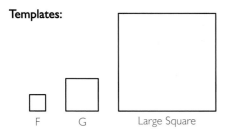

F   G   Large Square

PATCH SHAPES

The quilt centre is pieced from traditional ninepatch blocks which finish to 12in (30.5cm). They are pieced using 2 square patch shapes (Templates F and G). The smaller squares (Template F) are sub-pieced into fourpatch units and then arranged with the larger squares (Template G) to form the ninepatch blocks, paying special attention to the placement of the light fabric patches. The ninepatch blocks are then alternated with a large square (cut to size). The borders on this quilt are added in an unusual way with a series of horizontal borders, 2 of which are fussy cut to take advantage of the fabric design. Finally an inner and outer vertical border are added to complete the quilt.

CUTTING OUT

Template F: Cut 2½in (6.5cm) strips across the width of the fabric. Each strip will give you 16 patches per full width. Cut 104 in GP88PR and GP93GN.

Template G: Cut 4½in (11.5cm) strips across the width of the fabric. Each strip will give you 8 patches per full width. Cut 52 in GP94PU and 13 in GP93GN.

Large Square: Cut 12½in (31.75cm) strips across the width of the fabric. Each strip will give you 3 patches per full width. Cut 12½in (31.75cm) squares, cut 12 in GP94MG.

Horizontal Borders:

GP90OC: Cut 6 strips 2in (5cm) wide across the width of the fabric. Sew a full width strip to a half width strip to make a border 60½in

x 2in (153.75cm x 5cm), make 4. Make sure that the chevron design runs continuously as shown in the photograph. These borders will be aligned in their final placement so try to ensure the 4 borders are the same.
GP86RD: Cut 3 strips 4½in (11.5cm) wide across the width of the fabric. Join as necessary and cut 2 borders 60½in x 4½in (153.75cm x 11.5cm).
GP93BK: Cut 3 strips 5½in (14cm) wide across the width of the fabric. Join as necessary and cut 2 borders 60½in x 5½in (153.75cm x 14cm).

Vertical Borders:

WBSFU: Cut 5 strips 2in (5cm) wide across the width of the fabric. Join as necessary and cut 2 borders 84½in x 2in (214.75cm x 5cm).
GP93BK: Cut 5 strips 4in (10.25cm) wide across the width of the fabric. Join as necessary and cut 2 borders 84½in x 4in (214.75cm x 10.25cm).

Binding: Cut 9yds (8.25m) of 2½in (6.5cm) wide bias binding in WBSLV.

Backing: Cut 2 pieces 39½in x 92in (100.5cm x 233.5cm) in backing fabric.

MAKING THE BLOCKS

Use a ¼in (6mm) seam allowance throughout. Using the quilt assembly diagram as a guide for fabric placement make 4 fourpatch units as shown in block assembly diagram a. Arrange the fourpatch units with the template G squares and stitch into 3 rows as shown in diagram b. Join the rows to complete the ninepatch block as shown in diagram c. The finished block can be seen in diagram d. Make a total of 13 blocks.

MAKING THE QUILT

Lay the ninepatch blocks out alternating with the large squares as shown in the quilt assembly diagram. Join into 5 rows, join the rows to complete the quilt centre.

Add the horizontal borders as shown in the quilt assembly diagram, making sure that the chevron stripes in the GP90OC fabric line up as shown in the photograph. Finally add the vertical borders as shown to complete the quilt.

FINISHING THE QUILT

Press the quilt top. Seam the backing pieces using a ¼in (6mm) seam allowance to form a piece approx. 78in x 92in (198cm x 233.5cm). Layer the quilt top, batting and backing and baste together (see page 138). Machine quilt as shown in the quilting diagram. Use invisible thread to quilt the seams that separate the ninepatch blocks and large squares, around the quilt centre and

Quilting Diagram

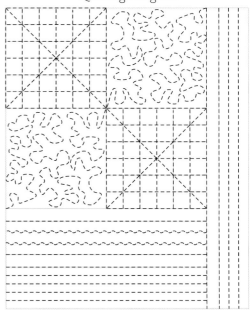

Block Assembly Diagrams

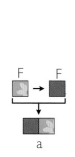

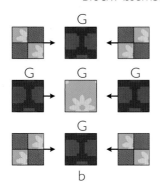

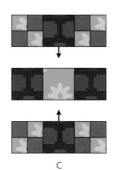

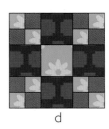

a   b   c   d

between the borders. Also quilt in the major seams within the ninepatch blocks. Use green thread for the diagonal lines through the light patches, forming a continuous diagonal grid over the surface of the quilt centre. Use purple thread to quilt a cross in the large dark squares in the ninepatch blocks and to quilt straight lines in the GP93BK fabric borders, 4 lines in the horizontal borders and 2 lines in the vertical borders. Using red thread the setting blocks are meander quilted following the fabric design, also quilt the GP86RD horizontal borders with 2 parallel serpentine lines. Trim the quilt edges and attach the binding (see page 139).

Quilt Assembly Diagram

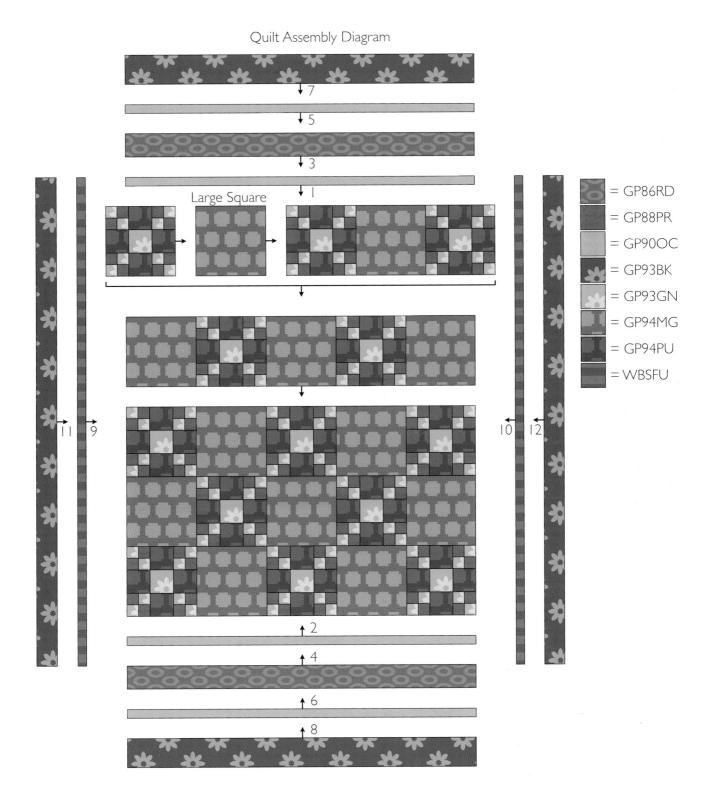

= GP86RD
= GP88PR
= GP90OC
= GP93BK
= GP93GN
= GP94MG
= GP94PU
= WBSFU

Large Square

103

Autumn Daze Quilt ★

PAULINE SMITH

This simple layout with a strong diagonal element looks good in rich, earthy shades.

SIZE OF QUILT

The finished quilt will measure approx. 76in x 88in (193cm x 223.5cm).

MATERIALS

Patchwork and Border Fabrics:

PAPERWEIGHT

Paprika   GP20PP: ½yd (45cm)

SPOT

Brown   GP70BR: ¼yd (25cm)
Grey   GP70GY: ½yd (45cm)

ASHA

Lime   GP75LM: ½yd (45cm)

LICHEN

Brown   GP76BR: ⅜yd (35cm)
Lilac   GP76LI: ⅜yd (35cm)

FLOWER DOT

Red   GP87RD: 1⅜yds (1.3m) incl. border

STAR FLOWER

Prune   GP88PR: ⅜yd (35cm)
Sepia   GP88SE: ½yd (45cm)

ASIAN CIRCLES

Orange   GP89OR: ½yd (45cm)

MILLEFIORE
Orange   GP92OR: 1⅞yds (1.7m)
                incl. border
BUBBLE FLOWER
Dusk   GP97DU: ⅜yd (35cm)
Teal   GP97TE: ½yd (45cm)
WOOD EAR
Red   GP99RD: ½yd (45cm)
BEGONIA LEAVES
Pastel   PJ18PT: ¼yd (25cm)
WOVEN MULTI STRIPE
Purple   WMSPU: ¼yd (25cm)

Backing Fabric: 6⅛yds (5.6m)
We suggest these fabrics for backing:
PAPER FANS Brown, GP57BR
LICHEN Brown, GP76BR
BUBBLE FLOWER Dusk, GP97DU

Binding:
STAR FLOWER
Prune   GP88PR: ¾yd (70cm)
Batting:
84in x 96in (213.5cm x 244cm).

Quilting Thread:
Deep coral hand or machine quilting thread.

Templates:

PATCH SHAPES
The centre of this quilt is pieced from 2
alternating blocks, Block 1 uses a triangle
patch shape (Template L) and Block 2 a
rectangle patch shape (Template M). The
centre is then surrounded with an inner
border and outer border, each with corner
posts, cut to size.

CUTTING OUT
To prevent waste please cut the fabric in the
order stated.
Inner Border: Cut 7 strips 3in (7.5cm) wide
across the width of the fabric in GP87RD.
Join as necessary and cut 2 strips 3in x
72½in (7.5cm x 184.25cm) for the quilt sides
and 2 strips 3in x 60½in (7.5cm x 153.75cm)
for the quilt top and bottom.
Outer Border: Cut 8 strips 6in (15.25cm)
wide across the width of the fabric in
GP92OR. Join as necessary and cut 2 strips
6in x 77½in (15.25cm x 197cm) for the quilt
sides and 2 strips 6in x 65½in (15.25cm x
166.5cm) for the quilt top and bottom.
Template L: Cut 6⅞in (17.5cm) strips across

the width of the fabric. Each strip will give
you 10 patches per full width. Cut 11 in
GP75LM, 10 in GP97DU, GP99RD, 9 in
GP20PP, GP88SE, GP18PT, 8 in GP70BR,
GP70GY, GP76BR, GP87RD, GP97TE,
WMSPU, 7 in GP89OR and GP92OR.
Template M: Fabric GP75LM only, use
leftover strip from template L, trim to 6½in
(16.5cm) wide, cut 6 rectangles.
For all other fabrics: Cut 3½in (9cm) strips
across the width of the fabric. Each strip will
give you 6 patches per full width. Cut 15 in
GP88PR, 13 in GP76LI, 12 in GP87RD, 11 in
GP99RD, 10 in GP20PP, GP88SE, GP89OR, 9
in GP97TE, 8 in GP70GY, 6 in GP76BR,
GP97DU and 4 in GP92OR.
Inner Border Corner Posts: Using leftover
strip from template L cut 4 x 3in (7.5cm)
squares in GP70BR.
Outer Border Corner Posts: Cut 4 x 6in
(15.25cm) squares in GP87RD.

Binding: Cut 9 strips 2½in (6.5cm) wide
across the width of the fabric in GP88PR.

Backing: Cut 2 pieces 40in x 96in (101.5cm
x 244cm), 2 pieces 40in x 5in (101.5cm x
12.75cm) and 1 piece 17in x 5in (43.25cm x
12.75cm) in backing fabric.

MAKING THE BLOCKS
Use a ¼in (6mm) seam allowance
throughout. Referring to the quilt assembly
diagram for fabric combinations take 2

template L triangles and join as shown in
block assembly diagram a. The finished Block
1 is shown in diagram b. Make 120. Next take
2 template M rectangles and join as shown in
block assembly diagram c. The finished Block
2 in shown in diagram d. Make 120.

MAKING THE QUILT
Lay out the blocks, alternating them as shown
in the quilt assembly diagram. Join into 12
rows of 10 blocks. Join the rows to complete
the quilt centre. Add the side inner borders
to the quilt centre. Join an inner border
corner post to each end of the top and
bottom inner borders then add to the quilt
centre. Join the outer border in the same
way to complete the quilt.

FINISHING THE QUILT
Press the quilt top. Seam the backing pieces
using a ¼in (6mm) seam allowance to form a
piece approx. 84in x 96in (213.5cm x
244cm). Layer the quilt top, batting and
backing and baste together (see page 138).
Hand or machine quilt using deep coral
quilting thread. Stitch in the ditch around
each block and also through the Block 2
centre seams, continuing across the Block 1
centres to make continuous lines across the
quilt centre. Also quilt in the main seams of
the borders and a line in the outer border
offset by 2in (5cm) from the inner seam.
Trim the quilt edges and attach the binding
(see page 139).

Block Assembly Diagrams

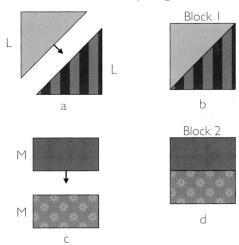

Quilt Assembly Diagram

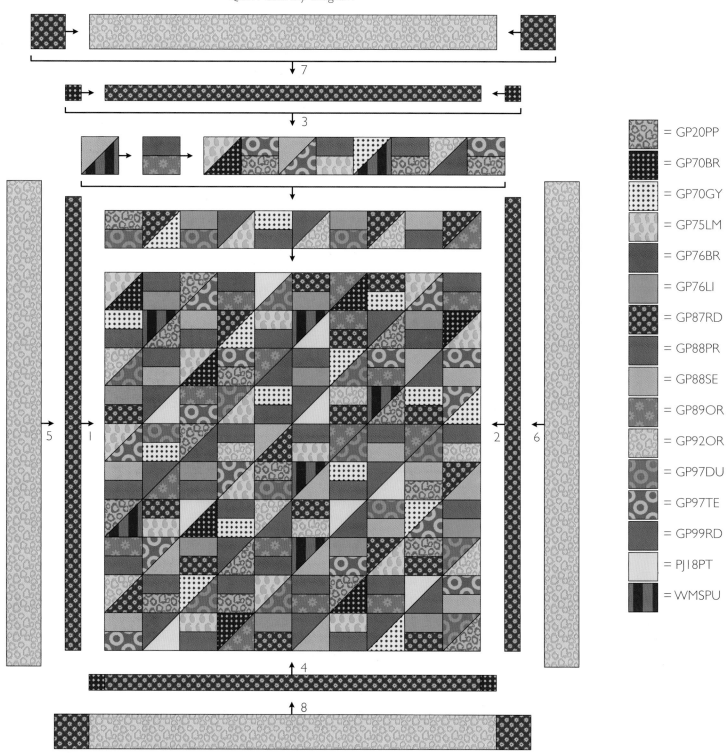

= GP20PP

= GP70BR

= GP70GY

= GP75LM

= GP76BR

= GP76LI

= GP87RD

= GP88PR

= GP88SE

= GP89OR

= GP92OR

= GP97DU

= GP97TE

= GP99RD

= PJI8PT

= WMSPU

Arrow Feathers ★★

PAM GOECKE DINNDORF

Careful cutting of luscious woven stripe fabrics produces a rich and exciting chevron effect. Handling all those bias edges is a bit tricky, but the finished quilt is well worth the effort!

SIZE OF QUILT
The finished quilt will measure approx.
52½in x 69in (133.5cm x 176cm).

MATERIALS
Patchwork and Border Fabrics:

HAZE STRIPE
Persimmon	S4481:	½yd (45cm)
Ginger	S4500:	⅝yd (60cm)
Pewter	S4515:	1yd (90cm)
Sunshine	S4519:	⅝yd (60cm)

SINGLE IKAT FEATHER
Curry	SIF01:	⅝yd (60cm)
Raspberry	SIF06:	⅝yd (60cm)

WOVEN TONE STRIPE
Citrus	WTSCN:	⅝yd (60cm)

Gold   WTSGD: ⅝yd (60cm)
Red   WTSRD: ¾yd (70cm)
Suede   WTSSD: ⅝yd (60cm)
Spice   WTSSI: ½yd (45cm)

Backing Fabric: 5yds (4.6m)
We suggest these fabrics for backing:
SHOT COTTON Nut, SC53
HAZE STRIPE Ginger, S4500
SINGLE IKAT FEATHER Raspberry, SIF06.

Binding:
SINGLE IKAT FEATHER
Raspberry   SIF06: ⅝yd (60cm)

Batting:
60in × 77in (152.5cm × 195.5cm)

Quilting Thread:
Toning machine quilting thread.

Templates:

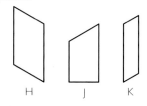

H   J   K

PATCH SHAPES
The centre of this quilt is pieced in vertical rows using a parallelogram patch shape (Template H) and a 'filler' patch shape (Template J). The centre is then surrounded with a simple inner border, then a pieced border using a second parallelogram patch shape (Template K), this border is trimmed to fit. Finally a simple outer border is added to complete the quilt. Important note: All the fabrics used in this quilt are reversible and the cutting instructions reflect this, however if you choose non reversible fabrics you will need to make additional 'reverse' templates and cut your fabric appropriately.

SPECIAL CUTTING NOTES
The Woven Tone Stripe fabrics used in this quilt have 3 different widths of stripe running along the length of the fabric. There are 2 sections of wide stripes at 12in (30.5cm) wide, 2 sections of medium stripes at 6in (15.25cm) wide and 2 sections of narrow stripes, 1 at 6in (15.25cm) wide and 1 at 3in

wide (7.5cm) (along the selvedge). Take note of the positioning of the different stripe widths by looking at the photograph, in the cutting instructions below we have stated how many of each stripe width to cut. We recommend making clear plastic templates for all 3 shapes so that the stripe direction, which is denoted by the arrows on the templates, can be cut accurately.

CUTTING OUT
First, please read the special cutting notes above. It is not appropriate to use our usual strip cutting method for this quilt as it would be very wasteful. After cutting the inner and outer borders we suggest drawing round all the required shapes into each fabric for the best fit and then cutting. Take careful note of the stripe direction as denoted by the arrows on the templates. Handle the cut patches carefully as the long sides will have bias edges.

Inner Border: Cut 6 strips 2¼in (5.75cm) wide across the width of the fabric in S4515. Join as necessary and cut 2 strips 2¼in × 61in (5.75cm × 155cm) for the quilt sides and 2 strips 2¼in × 47in (5.75cm × 119.5cm) for the quilt top and bottom. These are oversized and will be trimmed later.
Outer Border: Cut 7 strips 2¼in (5.75cm) wide across the width of the fabric in S4500. Join as necessary and cut 2 strips 2¼in × 68in (5.75cm × 173cm) for the quilt sides and 2 strips 2¼in × 54½in (5.75cm × 138.5cm) for the quilt top and bottom. These are oversized and will be trimmed later.
Template H: Cut 11 in SIF01, WTSRD (4 wide stripe, 4 medium stripe, 3 narrow stripe), 9 in S4519, SIF06, WTSGD (5 wide stripe, 2 medium stripe, 2 narrow stripe), 8 in S4515, WTSCN (3 wide stripe, 3 medium stripe, 2 narrow stripe), WTSSD (2 wide stripe, 4 medium stripe, 2 narrow stripe), 6 in WTSSI (2 wide stripe, 4 medium stripe) and 5 in S4481.
Template J: Cut 4 in WTSSD (2 wide stripe, 2 medium stripe), 3 in S4481, SIF01, WTSGD (1 wide stripe, 1 narrow stripe), 2 in S4515, S4519, SIF06, WTSRD (1 wide stripe, 1 medium stripe), WTSSI (1 medium stripe, 1 narrow stripe) and 1 in WTSCN (wide stripe).

Template K: Cut 5 in S4519, WTSCN (3 wide stripe, 1 medium stripe, 1 narrow stripe), WTSGD (1 wide stripe, 3 medium stripe, 1 narrow stripe), WTSRD (1 wide stripe, 3 medium stripe, 1 narrow stripe), WTSSD (1 wide stripe, 2 medium stripe, 2 narrow stripe), 4 in SIF06, 3 in S4481, 2 in SIF01 and WTSSI (1 wide stripe, 1 narrow stripe).

Binding: Cut 7⅛yds (6.5m) of 2½in (6.5cm) wide bias binding in SIF06.

Backing: Cut 2 pieces 39in × 60in (99cm × 152.5cm) in backing fabric.

MAKING THE QUILT
Use a ¼in (6mm) seam allowance throughout. Referring to the quilt assembly diagram for fabric placement lay out the template H parallelograms in vertical rows, filling in with the template J 'filler' shapes at the top and bottom of each row. Join the patches to form 12 rows. Join the rows to form the quilt centre. Tip: When joining the rows stitch the first seam from top to bottom, the next from bottom to top and so on alternating the stitch direction for each row. This is particularly helpful when joining bias edges as it helps to prevent distortion.

ADDING THE BORDERS
Add the side inner borders, trimming to fit exactly, then the top and bottom inner borders, again trimming to fit. The next border is pieced using the template K parallelograms. Make 2 borders of 10 patches for the quilt sides, add to the quilt and trim to fit. Make 2 borders of 8 patches for the quilt top and bottom, add to the quilt and trim to fit. Finally add the outer border in the same way as the inner border to complete the quilt.

FINISHING THE QUILT
Press the quilt top. Seam the backing pieces using a ¼in (6mm) seam allowance to form a piece approx. 60in × 77in (152.5cm × 195.5cm). Layer the quilt top, batting and backing and baste together (see page 138). Using toning machine quilting thread stitch in the ditch throughout the quilt centre and in the main seams of all the borders. Trim the quilt edges and attach the binding (see page 139).

Quilt Assembly Diagram

Outer Border

Pieced Border, trim to fit

Inner Border

Trim to fit

K

J

K

H

	= S4481		= SIF01		= WTSRD
	= S4500		= SIF06		= WTSSD
	= S4515		= WTSCN		= WTSSI
	= S4519		= WTSGD		

Incredible Stripes Quilt ★

SALLY DAVIS

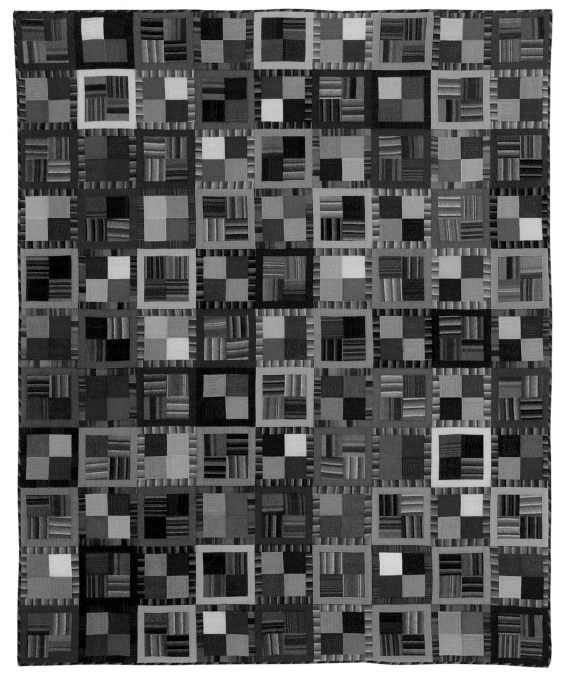

The jewel colours of Shot Cotton fabrics glow against the profusion of subtle stripes in this sumptuous quilt.

SIZE OF QUILT
The finished quilt will measure approx. 72in x 88in (183cm x 223.5cm).

MATERIALS
The instructions for this quilt are less formal than usual. We have included a list of all the fabrics Sally used and total requirements for Shot Cottons and Stripes, a ¼ yard (25cm) of most fabrics is plenty, and some have only been used in very small quantities, so this a great opportunity to use up scraps. When choosing your fabric selection, remember to include some bright 'sharp' colours to add lift.

Patchwork Fabrics:
SHOT COTTON: Buy a total of 4½yds (4.1m). These fabrics were included in Sally's quilt:

SHOT COTTON	
Persimmon	SC07
Raspberry	SC08
Tangerine	SC11
Chartreuse	SC12
Lavender	SC14
Mustard	SC16
Lichen	SC19
Pine	SC21

Grass	SC27
Watermelon	SC33
Sunshine	SC35
Jade	SC41
Lime	SC43
Cobalt	SC45
Aegean	SC46
Grape	SC47
Forget–Me–Not	SC51
Viridian	SC55
Moss	SC56
Caramel	SC59
Terracotta	SC61
Butter	SC64
Mint	SC65
Pool	SC71
Mulberry	SC73
Vermillion	SC74
Aqua	SC77

STRIPE FABRICS: Buy a total of 4½yds (4.1m).
These fabrics were included in Sally's quilt:

HAZE STRIPE

Aegean	S4491
Denim Blue	S4502
Ginger	S4500
Grape	S4504
Green	S4516
Lilac	S4470
Navy	S4496
Pine	S4490
Purple	S4498

WOVEN BOLD STRIPE

Fuchsia	WBSFU
Gold	WBSGD
Lavender	WBSLV
Teal	WBSTE

WOVEN MULTI STRIPE

Brown	WMSBR
Fuchsia	WMSFU
Green	WMSGN
Indigo	WMSIN
Purple	WMSPU
Teal	WMSTE

Backing Fabric: 5¾yds (5.3m)
Any of the fabrics used in the quilt would be suitable for backing.

Binding:
WOVEN MULTI STRIPE
Indigo   WMSIN: ¾yd (70cm)

Batting:
80in × 96in (203cm × 244cm)

Quilting Thread:
Toning machine quilting thread.

Templates:

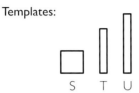

S   T   U

PATCH SHAPES
Pieced four patch blocks using a square patch (Template S) are each surrounded by a narrow border (Templates T and U). The blocks are made in 2 colour combinations, stripe four patch centres with shot cotton borders and shot cottons four patch centres with stripe borders.

CUTTING OUT
Template S: Cut 3½in (9cm) strips across the width of the fabric. Each strip will give you 11 patches per full width. Cut 200 in stripe fabrics and 196 in shot cotton fabrics.
Note: The border around each four patch block is pieced in the same fabric, so cut sets of borders (2 × template T and 2 × template U = 1 set) accordingly.
Template T: Cut 1½in (3.75cm) strips across the width of the fabric. Each strip will give you 6 patches per full width. Cut 100 in shot cotton fabrics and 98 in stripe fabrics.
Template U: Cut 1½in (3.75cm) strips across the width of the fabric. Each strip will give you 4 patches per full width. Cut 100 in shot cotton fabrics and 98 in stripe fabrics.

Binding: Cut 9¼yds (8.5m) of 2½in (6.5cm) wide bias binding in WMSIN.

Backing: Cut 2 pieces 40in × 96in (101.5cm × 244cm) in backing fabric.

MAKING THE BLOCKS
Use a ¼in (6mm) seam allowance throughout. The blocks are made in 2 colour combinations, stripe four patch centres with shot cotton borders (Block 1) and shot cottons four patch centres with stripe borders (Block 2). The border around each four patch block is pieced in the same fabric. Piece a total of 50 × Block 1 and 49 × Block 2 following the block assembly diagrams.

MAKING THE QUILT
Lay out the blocks alternating Blocks 1 and 2 throughout the quilt. Make sure you distribute the colours spreading the 'sharp' colours throughout to add lift. Join the blocks into 11 rows of 9 blocks per row. Join the rows to complete the quilt.

FINISHING THE QUILT
Press the quilt top. Seam the backing pieces using a ¼in (6mm) seam allowance to form a piece approx. 80in × 96in (203cm × 244cm). Layer the quilt top, batting and backing and baste together (see page 138). Machine quilt using toning quilting thread, stitch in the ditch between all the blocks and then free motion quilt in the four patch blocks using a selection of spirals, squared spirals and meander quilting. Trim the quilt edges and attach the binding (see page 139).

Block Assembly Diagrams

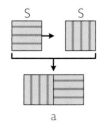

a

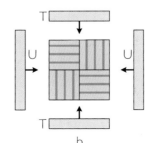

b

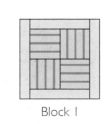

Block 1

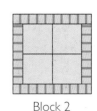

Block 2

Quilt Assembly Diagram

= Shot Cottons = Stripes

Summer Tumbling Blocks Quilt ★★

LIZA PRIOR LUCY

Brandon's new fabric line came just in time for me to make a quilt in my other favourite pattern, Tumbling Blocks. The boldness of these contemporary prints called out for a large scale version. The colours of Portmeirion determined the palette. Mixing fussy florals and bold graphic prints was a real treat.

SIZE OF QUILT
The finished quilt will measure approx.
72in × 82in (183cm × 208cm).

MATERIALS
Patchwork and Border Fabrics:
RIPPLE
Lavender	BM02LV:	⅜yd (35cm)
Pastel	BM02PT:	⅜yd (35cm)
Pink	BM02PK:	⅜yd (35cm)

WAVES
Lipstick	BM04LP:	⅜yd (35cm)
Pastel	BM04PT:	⅜yd (35cm)

DAPPLE
Blue	BM05BL:	⅜yd (35cm)
Pink	BM05PK:	⅜yd (35cm)

JAZZ
Pink	BM06PK:	2¼yds (2.1m) incl. borders
Red	BM06RD:	⅜yd (35cm)

FISH LIPS
Pastel	BM07PT:	⅜yd (35cm)
Red	BM07RD:	⅜yd (35cm)

HENNA
Blue	GP96BL:	⅜yd (35cm)
Duck Egg	GP96DE:	⅜yd (35cm)

BUBBLE FLOWER
Blue	GP97BL:	⅜yd (35cm)
Pink	GP97PK:	⅜yd (35cm)

WALTZING MATILDA
Pastel	PJ22PT:	⅜yd (35cm)
Yellow	PJ22YE:	⅜yd (35cm)

TROPICAL
Celadon	PJ23CD:	⅜yd (35cm)
Pink	PJ23PK:	⅜yd (35cm)

TULIP MANIA
Pastel	PJ24PT:	⅜yd (35cm)

LAYERED LEAVES
Celadon	PJ26CD:	⅜yd (35cm)

Backing Fabric: 5½yds (5m)
We suggest these fabrics for backing:
HENNA Duck Egg; GP96DE
WALTZING MATILDA Pastel, PJ22PT
TROPICAL Pink, PJ23PK

Binding:
HENNA		
Duck Egg	GP96DE:	¾yd (70cm)

Batting:
80in × 90in (203cm × 228.5cm).

Quilting Thread:
Toning hand or machine quilting thread.

Templates:

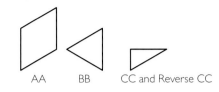

AA   BB   CC and Reverse CC

PATCH SHAPES
This classic Tumbling Blocks pattern is made
the easy way by splitting the top of each
tumbling block into 2 triangles, then piecing
the quilt in vertical rows. It is made using 1
diamond patch (Template AA), 1 equilateral
triangle (Template BB) and 1 right angle
triangle to fill the column ends (Template CC
and Reverse CC). The quilt is surrounded
with a border which is fussy cut to emphasise
the bold zigzag design of the 'Jazz' fabric.

CUTTING OUT
Cut the fabric in the order stated to prevent
waste.
Borders: In fabric BM06PK cut 2 strips down
the length of the fabric parallel with the
selvedge, 5½in × 73in (14cm × 185.5cm) for
the side borders, these are a little oversized
and will be trimmed to fit later. The remaining
fabric will be approx. 29in (73.5cm) wide, for
the top and bottom borders cut 2 sets of 3
strips 5½in (14cm) wide across the width of
the remaining fabric, so that when they are
joined the pattern will match and run
correctly across the width. There is plenty of
fabric allowed to fussy cut these strips. Join
the strips to make 2 borders 5½in × 73½in
(14cm × 186.5cm) again, these are a little
oversized and will be trimmed to fit later.
Reserve the remaining fabric for template
AA.
Template AA: Cut 5in (12.75cm) strips
across the width of the fabric. Each strip will
give you 6 diamonds per full width. Cut 10 in
BM02PT, BM04LP, BM05BL, BM07PT, PJ22YE,
PJ24PT, 9 in BM02PK, BM06PK, BM07RD,
PJ26CD, 8 in BM06RD, PJ22PT, 7 in BM04PT
and GP96BL. Reserve leftover fabric for
template CC and reverse CC.

Template BB: Cut 5¼in (13.25cm) strips
across the width of the fabric. Each strip will
give you 12 triangles per full width. Cut 20 in
PJ23PK, 19 in GP96DE, 18 in BM02LV,
GP97BL, GP97PK, 17 in BM05PK and 16 in
PJ23CD. Reserve leftover fabric for template
CC and reverse CC.
Template CC and Reverse CC: Using
leftover fabric from templates AA and BB, cut
2 in GP97BL, PJ22YE, PJ24PT, 1 in BM02LV,
BM05PK, GP96BL, GP96DE, GP97PK, PJ22PT,
PJ23CD and PJ26CD. Reverse the template
by flipping it over then cut 2 in BM02PK,
BM04LP, BM05PK, BM07RD, 1 in BM02LV,
BM04PT, GP96DE, GP97BL, GP97PK and
PJ23CD.

Binding: Cut 8 strips 2½in (6.5cm) wide
across the width of the fabric in GP96DE.

Backing: Cut 2 pieces 40in × 91in (101.5cm
× 231cm) in backing fabric.

MAKING THE QUILT
Use a ¼in (6mm) seam allowance
throughout. Using the quilt assembly diagram
as a guide for fabric placement lay out the
whole quilt, we suggest using a design wall for
this. Make sure that the template BB triangles
come together in the same fabrics to form
the diamonds at the top of each tumbling
block. Carefully separate the patches into 14
vertical rows and piece each in order. Check
placement after each row is pieced to ensure
the pattern is correct. Join the rows to
complete the quilt centre. Add the side
borders, trimming to fit exactly, then the top
and bottom borders, again trimming to fit, to
complete the quilt.

FINISHING THE QUILT
Press the quilt top. Seam the backing
pieces using a ¼in (6mm) seam allowance
to form a piece approx. 80in × 90in
(203cm × 228.5cm). Layer the quilt top,
batting and backing and baste together
(see page 138). Using toning machine
quilting thread meander quilt following
the fabric designs across the whole quilt.
Trim the quilt edges and attach the binding
(see page 139).

Quilt Assembly Diagram

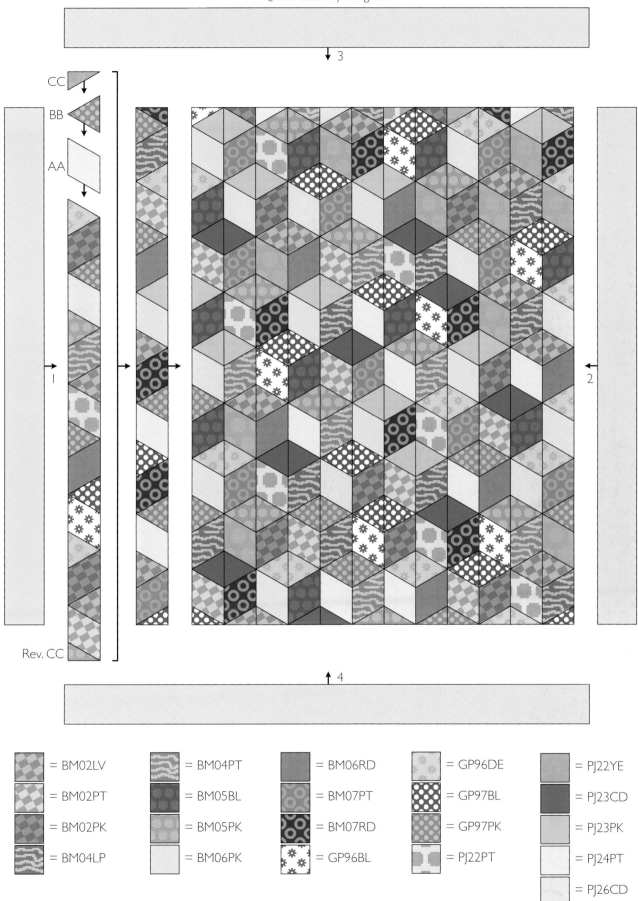

CC
BB
AA
Rev. CC

1
2
3
4

= BM02LV	= BM04PT	= BM06RD	= GP96DE	= PJ22YE
= BM02PT	= BM05BL	= BM07PT	= GP97BL	= PJ23CD
= BM02PK	= BM05PK	= BM07RD	= GP97PK	= PJ23PK
= BM04LP	= BM06PK	= GP96BL	= PJ22PT	= PJ24PT
				= PJ26CD

Hearts And Flowers Quilt ★★★

KIM MCLEAN

Kim's amazing appliqué quilt isn't as daunting to make as it might seem at first glance. This is due to the clever symmetry in the quilt layout and repetition of the motifs, plus you can choose your own favourite method of appliqué. It's a good opportunity to use scraps and leftovers from other Rowan projects.

SIZE OF QUILT
The finished quilt will measure approx.
78in × 78in (198cm × 198cm).

MATERIALS
Kim used many fabrics in her quilt, some in tiny quantities, so we have only listed the most prominent fabrics individually, the patchwork and appliqué fabrics are listed in 4 colourway categories. Many of the fabrics can be used in 2 or 3 categories due to the variety of colour in Kaffe's fabric designs, so don't be tied to the formula. This is also a good opportunity to use your own scraps from other Rowan projects!

Background Fabric:
ABORIGINAL DOTS
Ivory   GP71IV: 3⅞yds (3.6m)

Border 4:
ABORIGINAL DOTS
Periwinkle   GP71PE: 1⅜yds (1.25m)
(Also used for border 5 corner posts and binding)

Border 5:
DAHLIA BLOOMS
Pink   GP54PK: 1⅞yds (1.7m)

Appliqué Stems:
SHOT COTTON
Nut   SC53: ⅜yd (35cm)

Centre Panel Appliqué Hearts:
SPOT
Purple   GP70PU: ½yd (45cm)
STENCIL
Scarlet   GP79SC: ½yd (45cm)
SHOT COTTON
Forget–Me–Not SC51: ½yd (45cm)

Patchwork and Appliqué Fabrics:
Blues: Buy ¼yd (25cm) of each.
BIG BLOOMS Teal   GP91TE

MILLEFIORE Blue   GP92BL
LAKE BLOSSOMS Blue   GP93BL
CABBAGE PATCH Purple   GP94PU
Greens: Buy ¼yd (25cm) of each.
CLOISONNE Aqua   GP46AQ
ASIAN CIRCLES Green   GP89GN
LAKE BLOSSOMS Yellow   GP93YE
CABBAGE PATCH Green   GP94GN
Pinks: Buy ¼yd (25cm) of each.
LICHEN Lilac   GP76LI
BIG BLOOMS Duck Egg   GP91DE
BIG BLOOMS Turquoise   GP91TQ
Reds: Buy ¼yd (25cm) of each.
GUINEA FLOWER Apricot GP59AP
FLOATING FLOWERS Scarlet GP56SC
BEKAH Magenta   GP69MG
BEKAH Orange   GP69OR
PERSIMMON Red   GP74RD
LICHEN Rust   GP76RU
CLOUDS Red   GP86RD
BIG BLOOMS Red   GP91RD
LAKE BLOSSOMS Red   GP93RD

Backing Fabric: 6yds (5.5m)
We suggest these fabrics for backing:
TURKISH DELIGHT Red, GP81RD
BIG BLOOMS Red, GP91RD
(Leftover fabric from backing can be used in the quilt).

Binding:
ABORIGINAL DOTS
Periwinkle   GP71PE: See above.

Batting:
86in × 86in (218.5cm × 218.5cm).

Quilting Thread:
Toning machine quilting thread.

Templates:

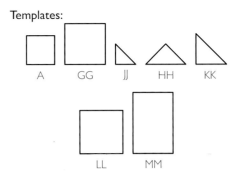

The appliqué shapes and appliqué designs on pages 131-135 are also used for this quilt.

PATCH SHAPES
This medallion style quilt is formed around a large centre panel with a series of 5 borders. The quilt is heavily appliquéd by hand, using a variety of methods including needle turn appliqué and freezer paper but you could choose to do the appliqué using adhesive web if you prefer. See the Patchwork Knowhow section at the back of the book for techniques.

The designs for appliqué on pages 131 & 132 are printed at 50% of true size, photocopy at 200% before using. The drawings for the centre panel and border 1 are for half the design, mirror to complete. We have also included full size templates for appliqué shapes where possible, please note that the appliqué shapes and designs DO NOT INCLUDE seam allowances. In addition to the printed full size appliqué shapes you will also need 6 card circles in the following diameter sizes, 1½in (3.75cm) and 2½in (6.5cm) for the centre panel, 3½in (9cm) and 4½in (11.5cm) for border 3 corner posts and 5½in (14cm) and 6½in (16.5cm) for border 5 corner posts.

The centre panel (cut to size) is appliquéd and we have provided a drawing of half the design. Border 1 (cut to size) has appliqué, for which we have provided a drawing of half the design. The corner posts for border 1 are also appliquéd (Template GG). Border 2 is pieced from 1 square (Template A) and 2 triangles (Templates HH and JJ), and also has appliqué. Border 3 is pieced from 1 square (Template LL), which has an appliquéd heart and 1 triangle (Template KK), which are pieced to form a 'square in a square' block. These are combined with 1 rectangle (Template MM) which has an appliquéd leaf. The corner posts of border 3 are also appliquéd and we have provided a drawing of the design. Border 4 is a simple border with corner posts, cut to size. Border 5 is

Block Assembly Diagrams

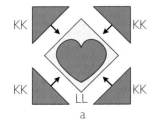

a

b

again a simple border, this time appliquéd corner posts, cut to size.

CUTTING OUT

Many of the appliqué background patches are cut oversized then trimmed once the appliqué is completed. We strongly recommend making plastic templates with motifs marked to make appliqué positioning easier. We have not given specific cutting instructions for the appliqué shapes as these are cut and appliquéd according to the designs.

Backing: Cut 2 pieces 40in × 86in (101.5cm × 218.5cm), 2 pieces 40in × 7in (101.5cm × 17.75cm) and 1 piece 7in × 7in (17.75cm × 17.75cm) in backing fabric, use leftover for patchwork and appliqué.

Centre Panel:
Cut 1 square 28in × 28in (71cm × 71cm) for the centre panel in GP71IV, this is oversized and will be trimmed later.

Border 1:
Cut 4 rectangles 28in × 7in (71cm × 17.75cm) in GP71IV, these are oversized and will be trimmed later. Cut 4 squares 7in × 7in (17.75cm × 17.75cm) in GP71IV, these are oversized and will be trimmed later using template GG.

Border 2:
Template HH: Cut 6¼in (16cm) strips across the width of the fabric, each full strip will give you 24 triangles. From the strips cut 6¼in (16cm) squares, then cut each square twice diagonally to make 4 triangles, using the template as a guide. This will ensure the long side of the triangle will not have a bias edge. Note: do not move the patches until both diagonals have been cut. Cut 48 triangles in GP71IV.

Template JJ: Cut 3⅜in (8.5cm) strips across the width of the fabric, each full strip will give you 22 triangles. Cut 32 triangles in GP71IV.

Template A: Cut 4in (10.25cm) strips across the width of the fabric, each full strip will give you 10 patches. Cut a total of 32 in various patchwork and appliqué fabrics, use the diagrams and photograph for help with fabric and colour placement.

Border 3:
Cut 4 squares 9in × 9in (22.75cm × 22.75cm) for corner posts in GP71IV. Cut 16 squares 7in × 7in (17.75cm × 17.75cm) in GP71IV for Template LL and 12 rectangles 7in × 9in (17.75cm × 22.75cm) in GP71IV for template MM, these are all oversized and will be trimmed later.

Template KK: Cut 4⅝in (11.75cm) strips across the width of the fabric, each full strip will give you 16 triangles. Cut a total of 64 triangles in various patchwork and appliqué fabrics, use the diagrams and photograph for help with fabric and colour placement.

Border 4:
Cut 6 strips across the width of the fabric, join as necessary and cut 4 strips 60½in × 2in (153.5cm × 5cm) in GP71PE. Also cut 4 corner posts 2in (5cm) square in green patchwork and appliqué fabric.

Border 5:
Cut 4 borders down the length of the fabric parallel with the selvedge 63½in × 8in (161.25cm × 20.25cm) in GP54PK. Also cut 4 corner posts 9in (22.75cm) square in GP71PE, these are oversized and will be trimmed later.

Binding: Cut 9 strips 2½in (6.5cm) wide across the width of the fabric in GP71PE.

MAKING THE CENTRE PANEL

Take the 28in × 28in (71cm × 71cm) square mark the centre vertical and horizontal lines by pressing, then sew large stitches by machine which will be removed when construction is complete. These lines will help you in marking the appliqué design and correct block dimensions later. Do the same for all appliqué background patches. Trace the centre panel appliqué design onto the right side of the fabric. With the scallops around the edge add about 1in (2.5cm) to the base after marking the finished line size. Appliqué the pieces, noting any layering. When complete press and using the centre lines as guides, on the wrong side mark the finished sewing line which will be a 25in (63.5cm) square, then add a ¼in (6mm) seam allowance to make a 25½in (64.75cm) square. Remove the excess fabric outside the seam allowance. You can also remove excess fabric from behind layered appliqué pieces if you wish.

MAKING AND ADDING THE BORDERS
Border 1:
Using the 4 rectangles 28in × 7in (71cm × 17.75cm), mark centre lines as above and appliqué pieces according to the border 1 appliqué design. When complete press and on the wrong side mark the finished sewing line which will be 25in × 5in (63.5cm × 12.75cm) rectangles, then add a ¼in (6mm) seam allowance to make 25½in × 5½in (64.75cm × 14cm) rectangles. Remove the excess fabric outside the seam allowance. Using the 4 squares 7in × 7in (17.75cm ×

17.75cm) appliqué the heart as shown on template GG. Once complete trim using template GG. Add the borders to the centre panel as shown in quilt assembly diagram 1.

Border 2:
Piece the borders and corner posts as shown in quilt assembly diagram 1 and add to the centre panel as shown. The appliqué circles are added AFTER border 3 is joined.

Border 3:
Using the 4 squares 7in × 7in (17.75cm × 17.75cm) appliqué the heart as shown on template LL. Once complete trim using template LL. Take the template KK triangles and piece 16 'square in a square' blocks as shown in block assembly diagram a, the finished block is shown in diagram b. Using the 4 rectangles 7in × 9in (17.75cm × 22.75cm) appliqué the leaves as shown on template MM. Once complete trim using template MM.

To make the corner posts use the 4 squares 9in × 9in (22.75cm × 22.75cm) mark centre lines as previously and appliqué pieces according to the border 3 appliqué design. When complete press and on the wrong side mark the finished sewing line which will be 7½in × 7½in (19cm × 19cm) squares, then add a ¼in (6mm) seam allowance to make 8in × 8in (20.25cm × 20.25cm) squares. Remove the excess fabric outside the seam allowance. Add the borders to the quilt as shown in quilt assembly diagram 2.

Border 2 again:
Go back to border 2. Take your plastic HH and JJ templates and cut out the marked circle shapes. Line up the template stitching lines with the sewn triangles in border 2 and mark the appliqué positions as shown in quilt assembly diagram 1 by drawing circles through the holes in the templates. Appliqué the circles and press.

Border 4:
Add border 4 as shown in quilt assembly diagram 2.

Border 5:
To make the corner posts use the 4 squares 9in × 9in (22.75cm × 22.75cm), mark centre lines as previously and appliqué pieces according to the border 5 appliqué design. When complete press and on the wrong side mark the finished sewing line which will be 7½in × 7½in (19cm × 19cm) squares,

then add a ¼in (6mm) seam allowance to make 8in × 8in (20.25cm × 20.25cm) squares. Remove the excess fabric outside the seam allowance. Add border 5 as shown in quilt assembly diagram 2 to complete the quilt.

FINISHING THE QUILT
Press the quilt top. Seam the backing pieces using a ¼in (6mm) seam allowance to form a piece approx. 86in × 86in (218.5cm × 218.5cm). Layer the quilt top, batting and backing and baste together

(see page 138). Using toning machine quilting thread, quilt as desired. Kim chose to outline and highlight the appliqué and stitch in the ditch in the patchwork and border seams. Trim the quilt edges and attach the binding (see page 139).

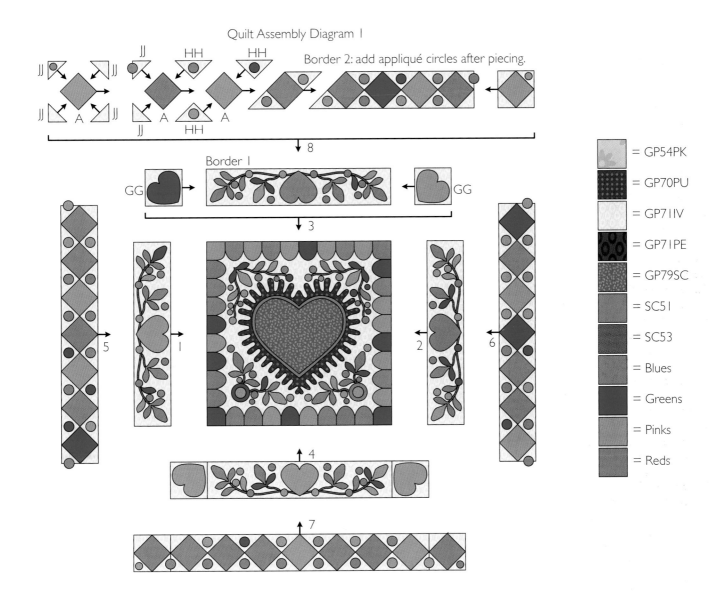

Quilt Assembly Diagram 1

= GP54PK
= GP70PU
= GP71IV
= GP71PE
= GP79SC
= SC51
= SC53
= Blues
= Greens
= Pinks
= Reds

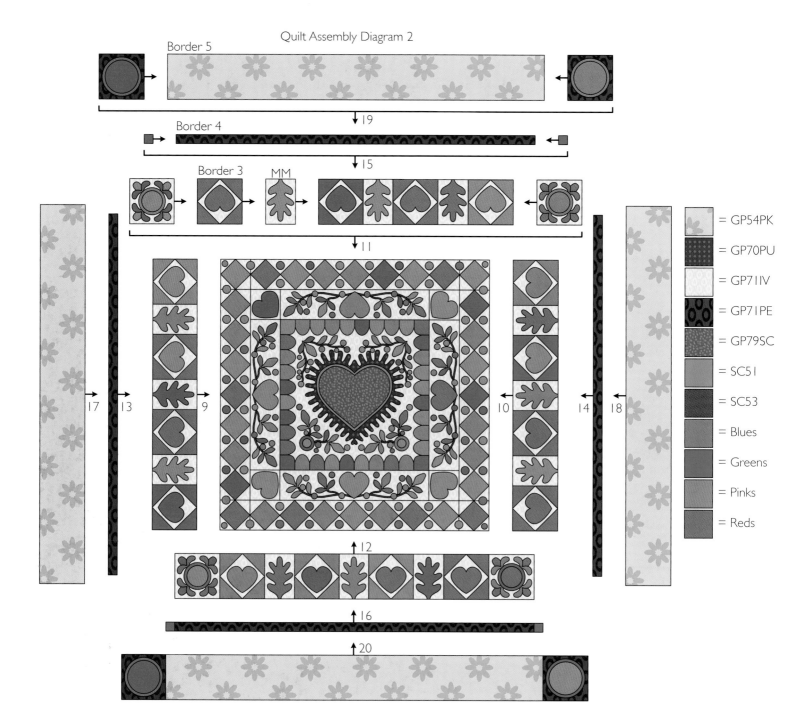

Quilt Assembly Diagram 2

Border 5

Border 4

Border 3   MM

17 13   9   10   14 18

12

16

20

= GP54PK

= GP70PU

= GP71IV

= GP71PE

= GP79SC

= SC51

= SC53

= Blues

= Greens

= Pinks

= Reds

Templates

Please refer to the individual quilt instructions for the templates required for each quilt as some templates are used in several quilts. The arrows on the templates should be lined up with the straight grain of the fabric, which runs either along the selvedge or at 90 degrees to the selvedge. Following the marked grain lines is important to prevent patches having bias edges along block and quilt edges which can cause distortion. In some quilts the arrows also denote stripe direction.

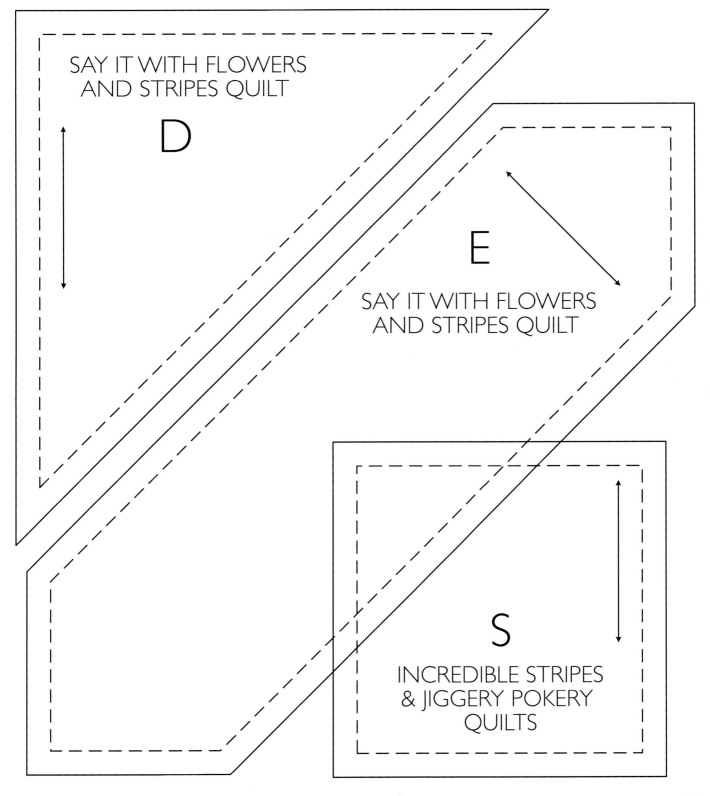

SAY IT WITH FLOWERS
AND STRIPES QUILT

D

E

SAY IT WITH FLOWERS
AND STRIPES QUILT

S

INCREDIBLE STRIPES
& JIGGERY POKERY
QUILTS

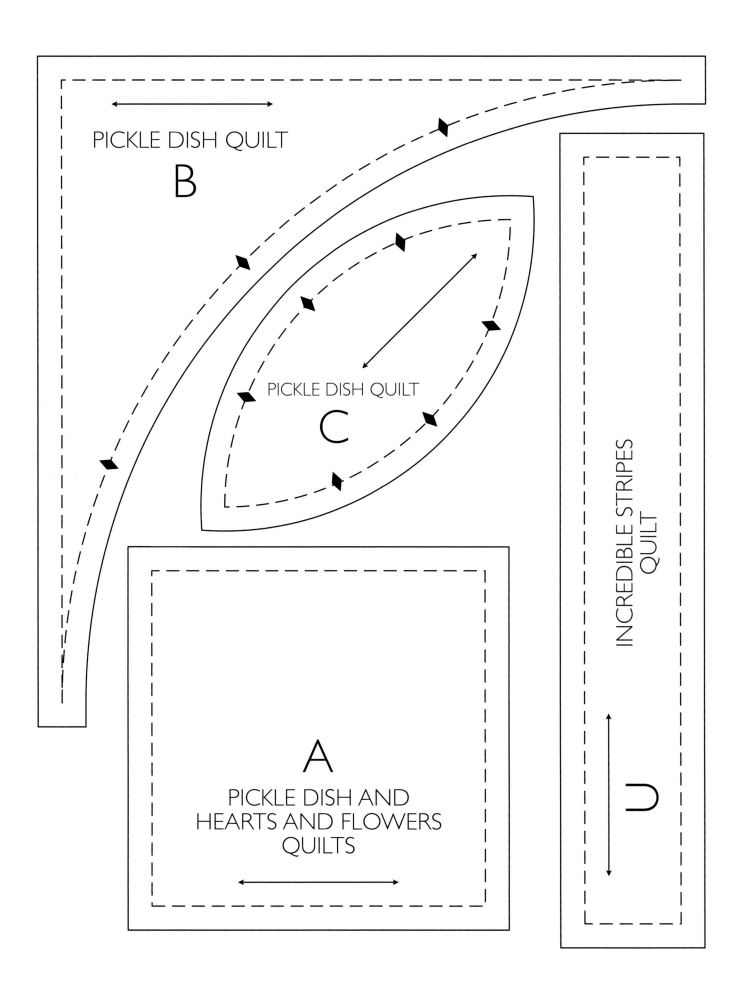

PICKLE DISH QUILT

B

PICKLE DISH QUILT

C

INCREDIBLE STRIPES QUILT

U

A

PICKLE DISH AND
HEARTS AND FLOWERS
QUILTS

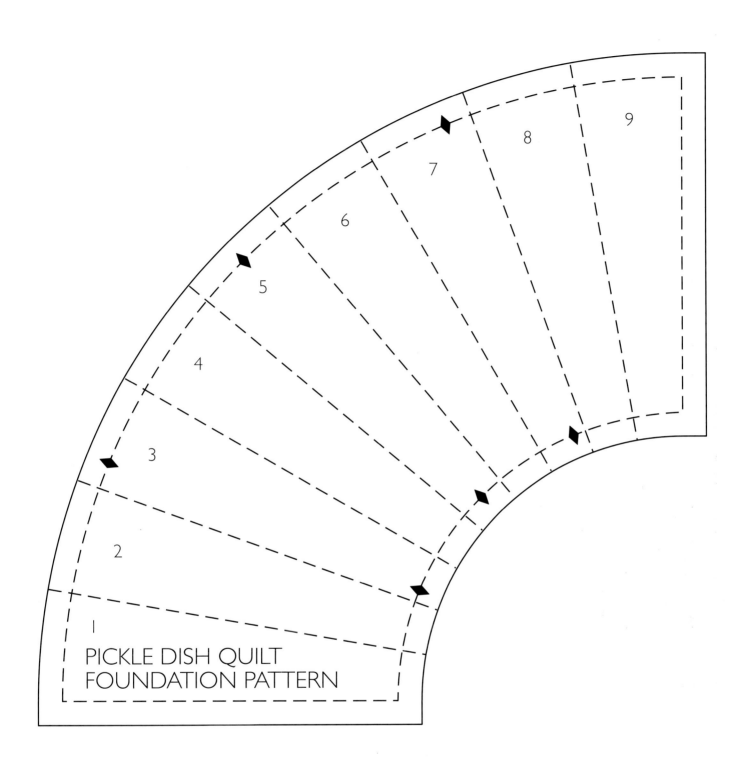

1

2

3

4

5

6

7

8

9

PICKLE DISH QUILT
FOUNDATION PATTERN

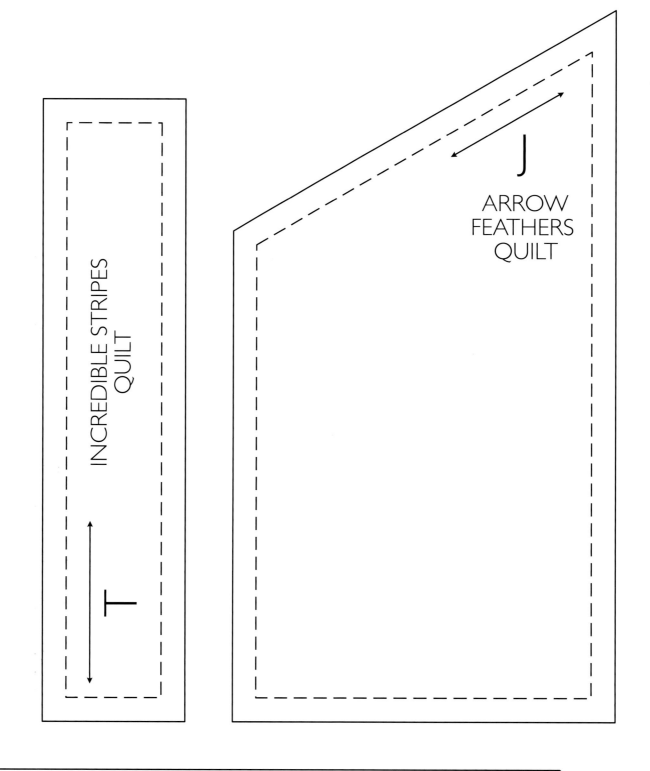

INCREDIBLE STRIPES
QUILT

T

J

ARROW
FEATHERS
QUILT

O

GOLD ITALIAN TILES &
PASTEL ITALIAN
TILES QUILTS

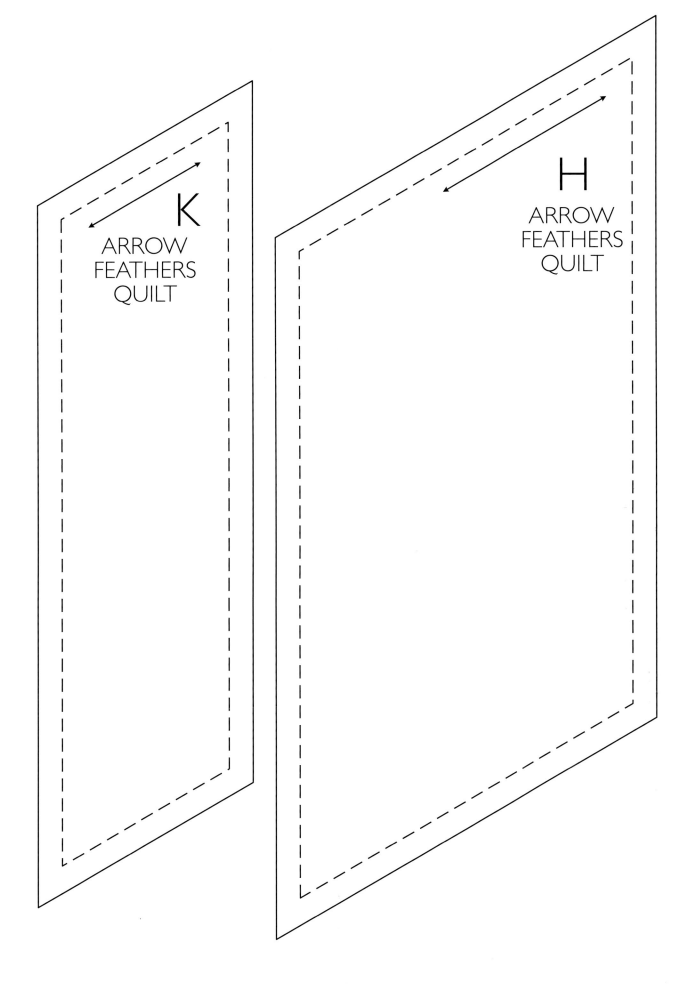

K

ARROW
FEATHERS
QUILT

H

ARROW
FEATHERS
QUILT

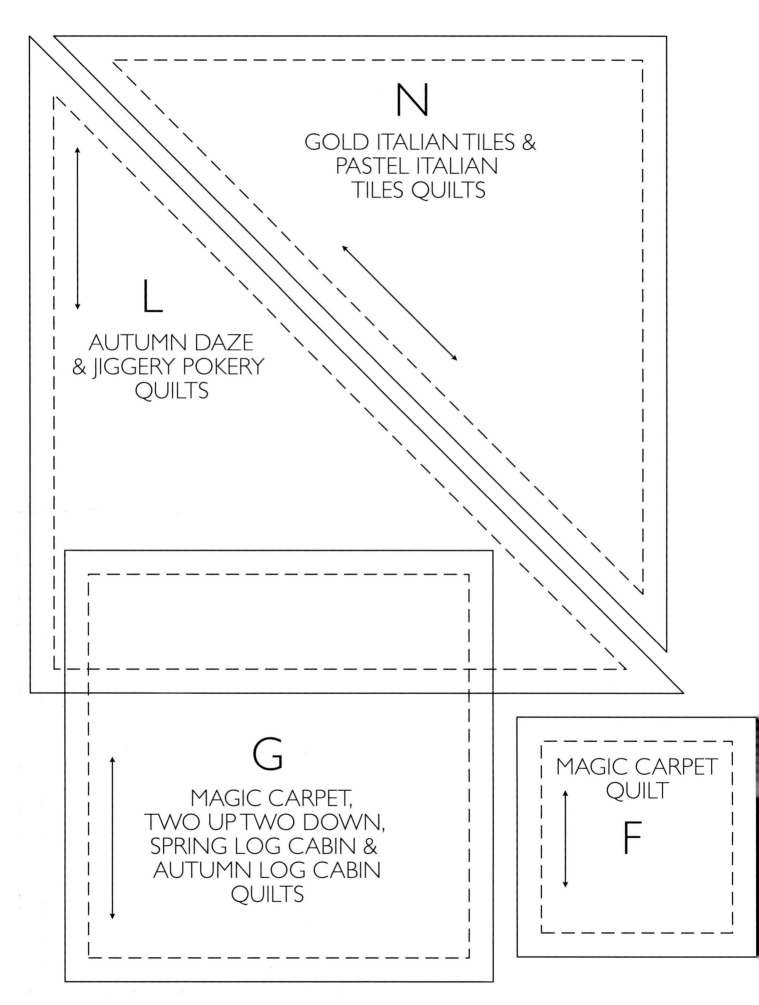

N

GOLD ITALIAN TILES &
PASTEL ITALIAN
TILES QUILTS

L

AUTUMN DAZE
& JIGGERY POKERY
QUILTS

G

MAGIC CARPET,
TWO UP TWO DOWN,
SPRING LOG CABIN &
AUTUMN LOG CABIN
QUILTS

MAGIC CARPET
QUILT

F

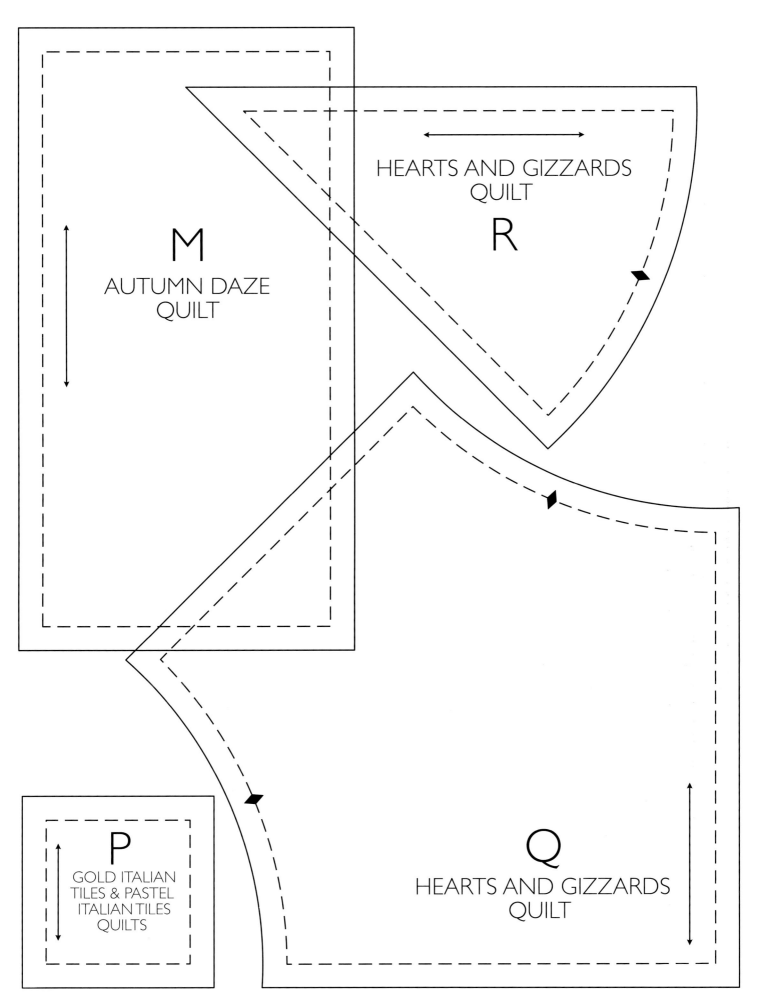

M
AUTUMN DAZE
QUILT

HEARTS AND GIZZARDS
QUILT
R

P
GOLD ITALIAN
TILES & PASTEL
ITALIAN TILES
QUILTS

Q
HEARTS AND GIZZARDS
QUILT

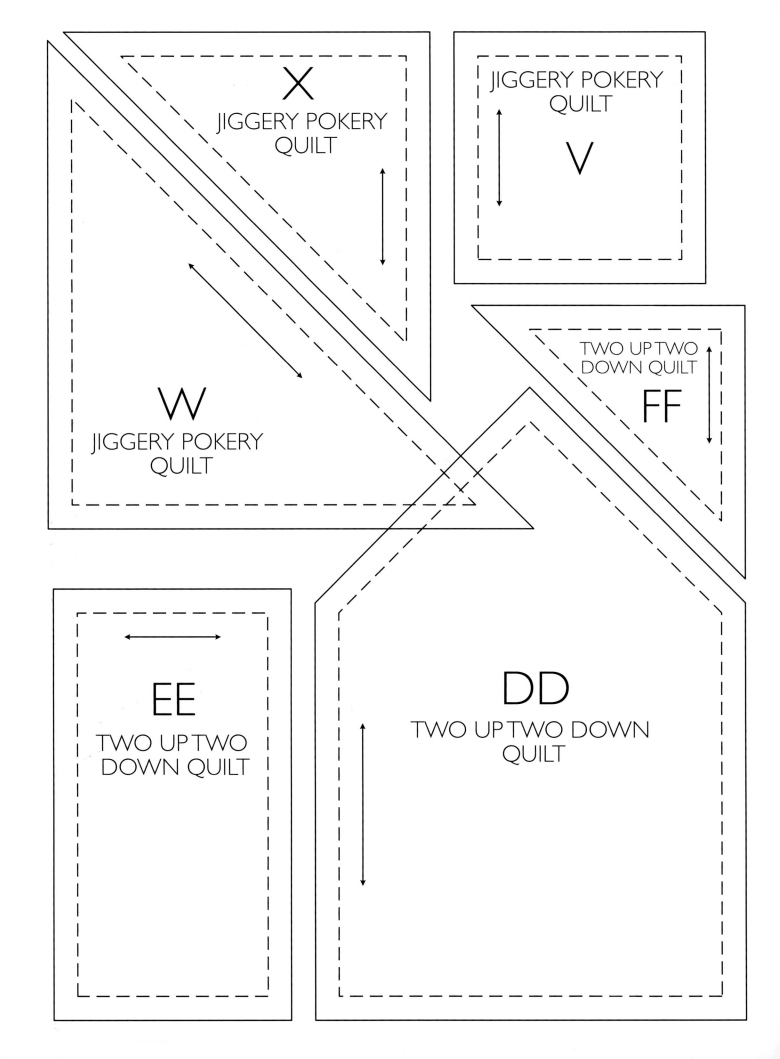

X
JIGGERY POKERY
QUILT

JIGGERY POKERY
QUILT
V

W
JIGGERY POKERY
QUILT

TWO UP TWO
DOWN QUILT
FF

EE
TWO UP TWO
DOWN QUILT

DD
TWO UP TWO DOWN
QUILT

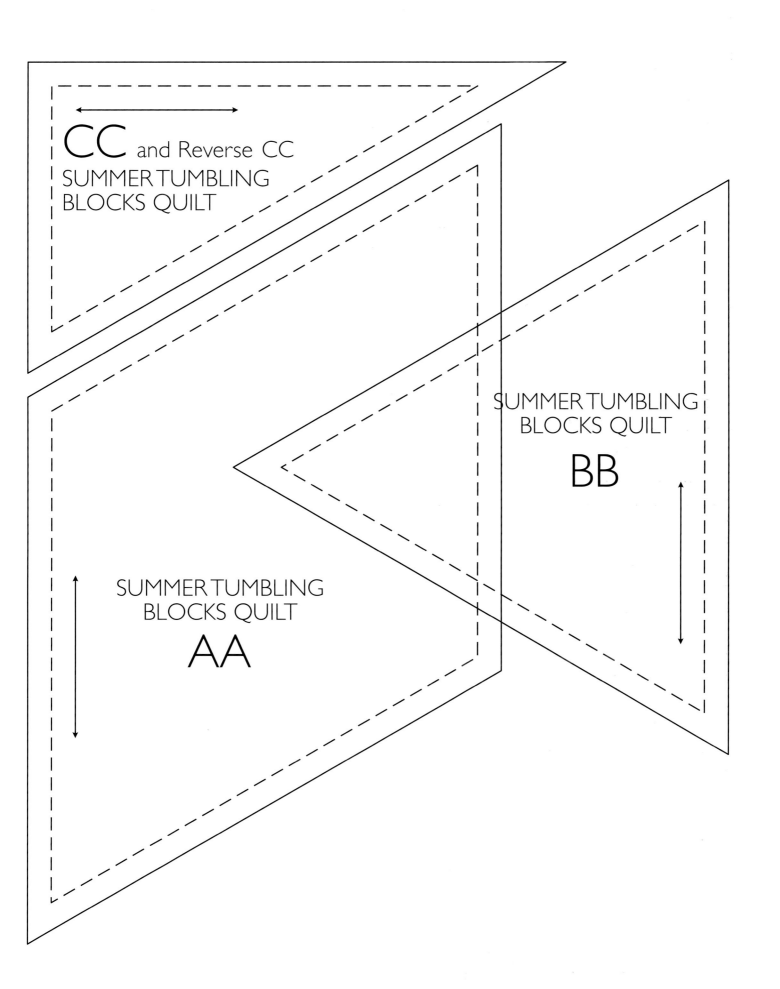

CC and Reverse CC
SUMMER TUMBLING
BLOCKS QUILT

SUMMER TUMBLING
BLOCKS QUILT
BB

SUMMER TUMBLING
BLOCKS QUILT
AA

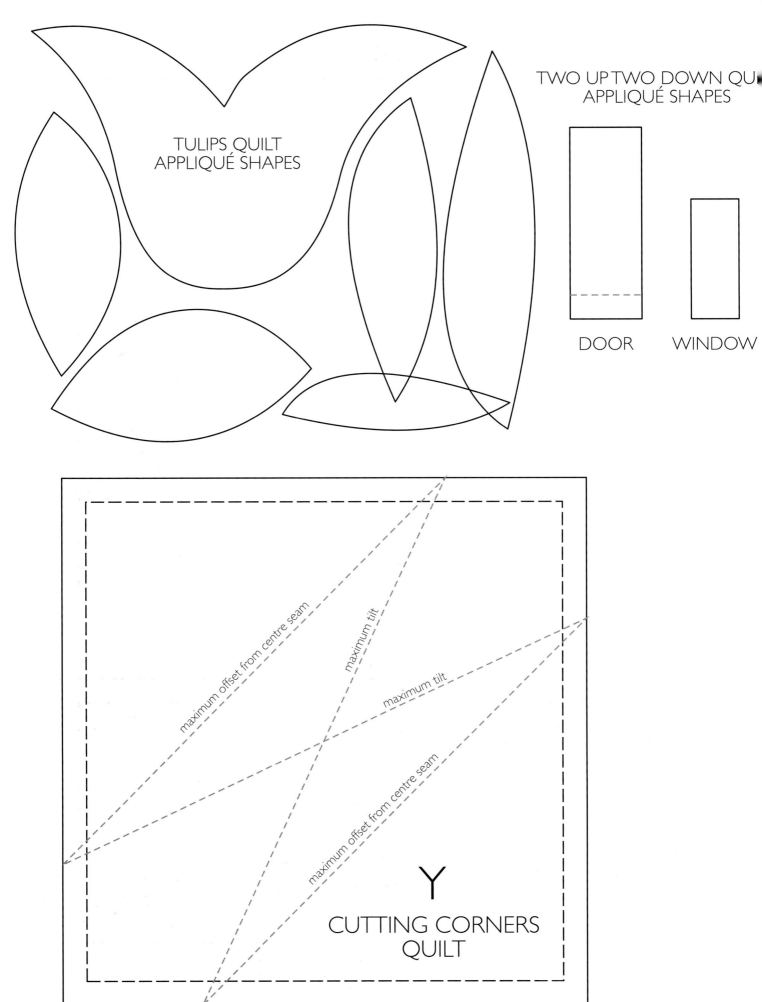

TULIPS QUILT
APPLIQUÉ SHAPES

TWO UP TWO DOWN QU
APPLIQUÉ SHAPES

DOOR WINDOW

maximum offset from centre seam

maximum tilt

maximum tilt

maximum offset from centre seam

Y
CUTTING CORNERS
QUILT

HEARTS AND FLOWERS QUILT

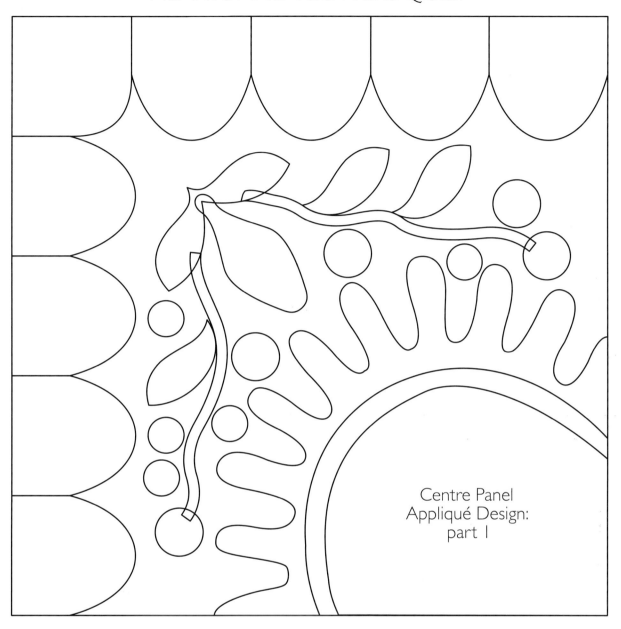

Centre Panel
Appliqué Design:
part 1

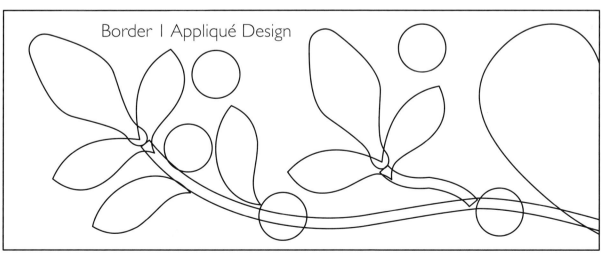

Border 1 Appliqué Design

All the designs on this page are printed at 50% of real
size. To use, scale up 200% on a photocopier.

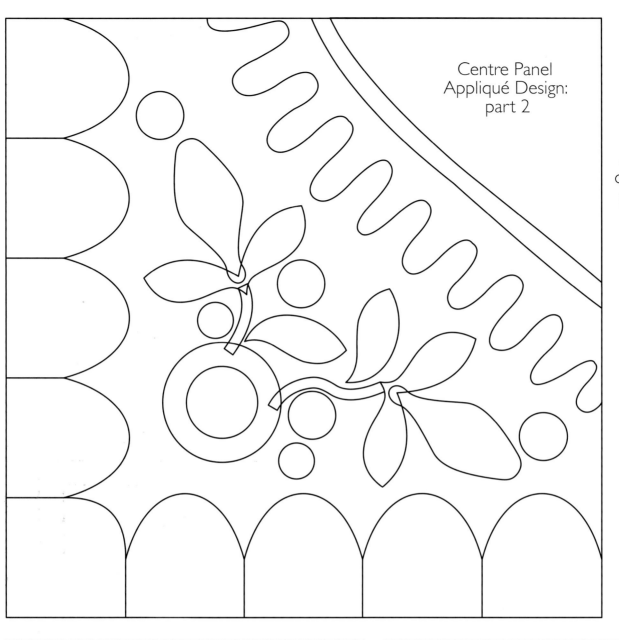

Centre Panel
Appliqué Design:
part 2

All the designs
on this page are
printed at 50%
of real size. To
use, scale up
200% on a
photocopier.

Border 3
Appliqué Design

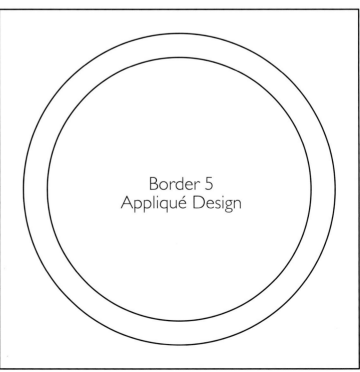

Border 5
Appliqué Design

HEARTS AND FLOWERS
QUILT FULL SIZE
APPLIQUÉ SHAPES

GG

HEARTS AND FLOWERS
QUILT

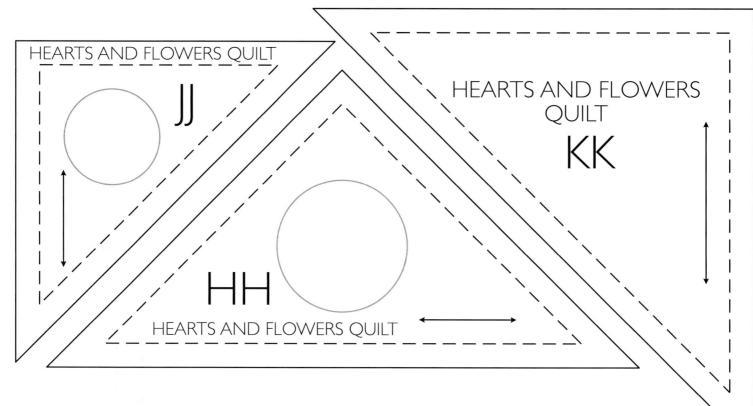

HEARTS AND FLOWERS QUILT

JJ

HEARTS AND FLOWERS
QUILT

KK

HH

HEARTS AND FLOWERS QUILT

LL

HEARTS AND FLOWERS
QUILT

MM

HEARTS AND FLOWERS
QUILT

Patchwork Know How

These instructions are intended for the novice quilt maker, providing the basic information needed to make the projects in this book, along with some useful tips.

Preparing the fabric

Prewash all new fabrics before you begin, to ensure that there will be no uneven shrinkage and no bleeding of colours when the finished quilt is laundered. Press the fabric whilst it is still damp to return crispness to it. All fabric requirements in this book are calculated on a 40in (101.5cm) usable fabric width to allow for shrinkage and selvedge removal.

Making templates

Transparent template plastic is the best material, it is durable and allows you to see the fabric and select certain motifs. You can also use thin stiff cardboard.

Templates for machine piecing

1 Trace off the actual–sized template provided either directly on to template plastic, or tracing paper, and then on to thin cardboard. Use a ruler to help you trace off the straight cutting line, dotted seam line and grain lines. Some of the templates in this book were too large to print at full size, they have therefore been printed at half real size. Photocopy them at 200% before using.

2 Cut out the traced off template using a craft knife, ruler and a self–healing cutting mat.

3 Punch holes in the corners of the template, at each point on the seam line, using a hole punch.

Templates for hand piecing

• Make a template as for machine piecing, but do not trace off the cutting line. Use the dotted seam line as the outer edge of the template.

• This template allows you to draw the seam lines directly on to the fabric. The seam allowances can then be cut by eye around the patch.

Cutting the fabric

On the individual instructions for each patchwork, you will find a summary of all the patch shapes used.
Always mark and cut out any border and binding strips first, followed by the largest patch shapes and finally the smallest ones, to make the most efficient use of your fabric. The border and binding strips are best cut using a rotary cutter.

Rotary cutting

Rotary cut strips are usually cut across the fabric from selvedge to selvedge, but some projects may vary, so please read through all the instructions before you start cutting the fabrics.

1 Before beginning to cut, press out any folds or creases in the fabric. If you are cutting a large piece of fabric, you will need to fold it several times to fit the cutting mat. When there is only a single fold, place the fold facing you. If the fabric is too wide to be folded only once, fold it concertina–style until it fits your mat. A small rotary cutter with a sharp blade will cut up to 6 layers of fabric; a large cutter up to 8 layers.

2 To ensure that your cut strips are straight and even, the folds must be placed exactly parallel to the straight edges of the fabric and along a line on the cutting mat.

3 Place a plastic ruler over the raw edge of the fabric, overlapping it about ½in (1.25cm). Make sure that the ruler is at right angles to both the straight edges and the fold to ensure that you cut along the straight grain. Press down on the ruler and wheel the cutter away from yourself along the edge of the ruler.

4 Open out the fabric to check the edge. Don't worry if it's not perfectly straight, a little wiggle will not show when the quilt is stitched together. Re–fold fabric, then place the ruler over the trimmed edge, aligning edge with the markings on the ruler that match the correct strip width. Cut strip along the edge of the ruler.

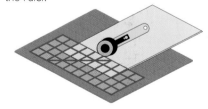

Using templates

The most efficient way to cut out templates is by first rotary cutting a strip of fabric the width stated for your template, and then marking off your templates along the strip, edge to edge at the required angle. This method leaves hardly any waste and gives a random effect to your patches.
A less efficient method is to fussy cut, where the templates are cut individually by placing them on particular motifs or stripes, to create special effects. Although this method is more wasteful it yields very interesting results.

1 Place the template face down, on the wrong side of the fabric, with the grain line arrow following the straight grain of the fabric, if indicated. Be careful though – check with your individual instructions, as some instructions may ask you to cut patches on varying grains.

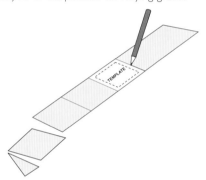

2 Hold the template firmly in place and draw around it with a sharp pencil or crayon, marking in the corner dots or seam lines. To save fabric, position patches close together or even touching. Don't worry if outlines positioned on the straight grain when drawn on striped fabrics do not always match the stripes when cut – this will add a degree of visual excitement to the patchwork!

3 Once you've drawn all the pieces needed, you are ready to cut the fabric, with either a rotary cutter and ruler, or a pair of sharp sewing scissors.

Basic hand and machine piecing

Patches can be joined together by hand or machine. Machine stitching is quicker, but hand assembly allows you to carry your patches around with you and work on them in every spare moment. The choice is yours. For techniques that are new to you, practise on scrap pieces of fabric until you feel confident.

Machine piecing

Follow the quilt instructions for the order in which to piece the individual patchwork blocks and then assemble the blocks together in rows.

1 Seam lines are not marked on the fabric, so stitch ¼in (6mm) seams using the machine needle plate, a ¼in (6mm) wide machine foot, or tape stuck to the machine as a guide. Pin two patches with right sides together, matching edges.

Set your machine at 10–12 stitches per inch (2.5cm) and stitch seams from edge to edge, removing pins as you feed the fabric through the machine.

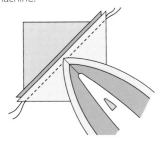

2 Press the seams of each patchwork block to one side before attempting to join it to another block.

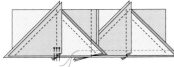

3 When joining rows of blocks, make sure that adjacent seam allowances are pressed in opposite directions to reduce bulk and make matching easier. Pin pieces together directly through the stitch line and to the right and left of the seam. Remove pins as you sew. Continue pressing seams to one side as you work.

Hand piecing

1 Pin two patches with right sides together, so that the marked seam lines are facing outwards.

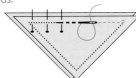

2 Using a single strand of strong thread, secure the corner of a seam line with a couple of back stitches.

3 Sew running stitches along the marked line, working 8–10 stitches per inch (2.5cm) and

ending at the opposite seam line corner with a few back stitches. When hand piecing never stitch over the seam allowances.

4 Press the seams to one side, as shown in machine piecing (Step 2).

Machine appliqué
Using adhesive web:

To make appliqué very easy you can use adhesive web, which comes attached to a paper backing sheet, to bond the motifs to the background fabric. There are 2 types of web available, the first keeps the pieces in place whilst they are stitched, the second permanently attaches the pieces so that no sewing is required. Follow steps 1 and 2 for the non–sew type and steps 1-3 for the type that requires sewing.

1 Trace the reversed appliqué design onto the paper side of the adhesive web leaving a 1/4in (6mm) gap between all the shapes. Roughly cut out the motifs 1/8in (3mm) outside your drawn line.

2 Bond the motifs to the reverse of your chosen fabrics. Cut out on the drawn line with very sharp scissors. Remove the backing paper by scoring in the centre of the motif carefully with a scissor point and peeling the paper away from the centre out, this prevents damage to the edges. Place the motifs onto the background noting any which may be layered. Cover with a clean cloth and bond with a hot iron (check instructions for temperature setting as adhesive web can vary depending on the manufacturer).

3 Using a contrasting or complimenting coloured thread in your machine, work small close zigzag stitches or a blanket stitch if your machine has one, around the edge of the motifs, the majority of the stitching should sit on the appliqué shape. When stitching up to points stop with the machine needle in the down position, lift the foot of your machine, pivot the work, lower the foot and continue to stitch. Make sure all the raw edges are stitched.

Hand appliqué

Good preparation is essential for speedy and accurate hand appliqué. The finger–pressing method is suitable for needle–turning application, used for simple shapes like leaves and flowers. Using a card template is the best method for bold simple motifs such as circles.

Finger–pressing:

1 To make your template, transfer the appliqué design on to stiff card using carbon paper, and cut out template. Trace around the outline of your appliquéd shape on to the right

side of your fabric using a well sharpened pencil. Cut out shapes, adding a ¼in (6mm) seam allowance all around by eye.

2 Hold shape right side up and fold under the seam, turning along your drawn line, pinch to form a crease. Dampening the fabric makes this very easy. When using shapes with 'points' such as leaves turn the seam allowance at the 'point' in first as shown in the diagram, then continue all round the shape. If your shapes have sharp curves you can snip the seam allowance to ease the curve. Take care not to stretch the appliqué shapes as you work.

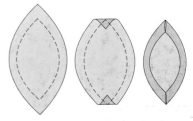

Card templates:

1 Cut out appliqué shapes as shown in step 1 of finger–pressing. Make a circular template from thin cardboard, without seam allowances.

2 Using a matching thread, work a row of running stitches close to the edge of the fabric circle. Place thin cardboard template in the centre of the fabric circle on the wrong side of the fabric.

3 Carefully pull up the running stitches to gather up the edge of the fabric circle around the cardboard template. Press, so that no puckers or tucks appear on the right side. Then, carefully pop out the cardboard template without distorting the fabric shape.

Straight stems:

Place fabric face down and simply press over the ¼in (6mm) seam allowance along each edge. You don't need to finish the ends of stems that are layered under other appliqué shapes. Where the end of the stem is visible simply tuck under the end and finish neatly.

Bias vines and stems:

1 Bias cut strips of fabric twice the desired finished width of the vine plus ½in (12mm). Fold the strip right side out matching the raw edges carefully and gently press. Lay the strip along the desired path and ease curves. Stitch the vine in place ¼in (6mm) from the raw edge as shown in the diagram, this can be done by hand or machine.

2 Fold the free edge of the vine over to cover the raw edges, again easing the curves, and slipstitch in place using a thread matching the vine.

Freezer paper:

1 Trace the appliqué shape onto the freezer paper and cut out. Make sure the coated side of the paper is next to the fabric and press onto the reverse. Cut out ¼in (6mm) outside the paper edge. Baste the seam allowance to the reverse, snipping the seam allowance at curves and points will allow it to lay flat.

2 Using a matching thread, bring the needle up from the back of the block into the edge of the shape and proceed to blind–hem in place. This is a stitch where the motifs appear to be held on invisibly. Bring the thread out from below through the folded edge of the motif, never on the top. Work around the complete shape, then turn the block over and remove the backing fabric from behind the appliqué shape leaving a ¼in (6mm) seam allowance. Remove basting threads and peel off the freezer paper.

Needle–turning application

1 Take the appliqué shape and pin in position. Stroke the seam allowance under with the tip of the needle as far as the creased pencil line, and hold securely in place with your thumb. Using a matching thread, bring the needle up from the back of the block into the edge of the shape and proceed to blind–hem in place. This is a stitch where the motifs appear to be held on invisibly. Bring the thread out from below through the folded edge of the motif, never on the top. The stitches must be worked small, even and close together to prevent the seam allowance from unfolding and frayed edges appearing. Try to avoid pulling the stitches too tight, as this will cause the motifs to pucker up. Work around the whole shape, stroking under each small section before sewing.

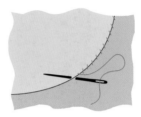

Quilting and finishing

When you have finished piecing your patchwork and added any borders, press it carefully. It is now ready for quilting.

Marking quilting designs and motifs

Many tools are available for marking quilting patterns, check the manufacturer's instructions for use and test on scraps of fabric from your project. Use an acrylic ruler for marking straight lines.

Stencils: Some designs require stencils, these can be made at home, by transferring the designs on to template plastic, or stiff cardboard. The design is then cut away in the form of long dashes, to act as guides for both internal and external lines. These stencils are a quick method for producing an identical set of repeated designs.

Preparing the backing and batting

• Remove the selvedges and piece together the backing fabric to form a backing at least 4in (10cm) larger all round than the patchwork top.

• For quilting choose a fairly thin batting, preferably pure cotton, to give your quilt a flat appearance. If your batting has been rolled up, unroll it and let it rest before cutting it to the same size as the backing.

• For a large quilt it may be necessary to join 2 pieces of batting to fit. Lay the pieces of batting on

a flat surface so that they overlap by approx. 8in (20cm). Cut a curved line through both layers.

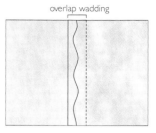

overlap wadding

• Carefully peel away the two narrow pieces and discard. Butt the curved cut edges back together. Stitch the two pieces together using a large herringbone stitch.

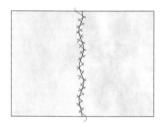

Basting the layers together

1 On a bare floor or large work surface, lay out the backing with wrong side uppermost. Use weights along the edges to keep it taut.

2 Lay the batting on the backing and smooth it out gently. Next lay the patchwork top, right side up, on top of the batting and smooth gently until there are no wrinkles. Pin at the corners and at the midpoints of each side, close to the edges.

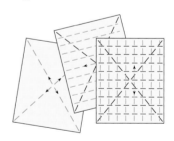

3 Beginning at the centre, baste diagonal lines outwards to the corners, making your stitches about 3in (7.5cm) long. Then, again starting at the centre, baste horizontal and vertical lines out to the edges. Continue basting until you have basted a grid of lines about 4in (10cm) apart over the entire quilt.

4 For speed, when machine quilting, some quilters prefer to baste their quilt sandwich layers together using rust–proof safety pins, spaced at 4in (10cm) intervals over the entire quilt.

Hand quilting

This is best done with the quilt mounted on a quilting frame or hoop, but as long as you have basted the quilt well, a frame is not essential. With the quilt top facing upwards, begin at the centre of the quilt and make even running stitches following the design. It is more important to make even stitches on both sides of the quilt than to make small ones. Start and finish your stitching with back stitches and bury the ends of your threads in the batting.

Machine quilting

• For a flat looking quilt, always use a walking foot on your machine for straight lines, and a darning foot for free–motion quilting.

• It's best to start your quilting at the centre of the quilt and work out towards the borders, doing the straight quilting lines first (stitch–in–the–ditch) followed by the free–motion quilting.

• When free motion quilting stitch in a loose meandering style as shown in the diagrams. Do not stitch too closely as this will make the quilt feel stiff when finished. If you wish you can include floral themes or follow shapes on the printed fabrics for added interest.

• Make it easier for yourself by handling the quilt properly. Roll up the excess quilt neatly to fit under your sewing machine arm, and use a table, or chair to help support the weight of the quilt that hangs down the other side.

Preparing to bind the edges

Once you have quilted or tied your quilt sandwich together, remove all the basting stitches. Then, baste around the outer edge of the quilt 1/4in (6mm) from the edge of the top patchwork layer. Trim the back and batting to the edge of the patchwork and straighten the edge of the patchwork if necessary.

Making the binding

1 Cut bias or straight grain strips the width required for your binding, making sure the grainline is running the correct way on your straight grain strips. Cut enough strips until you have the required length to go around the edge of your quilt.

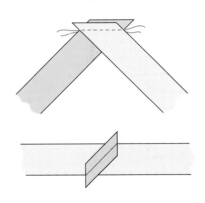

2 To join strips together, the two ends that are to be joined must be cut at a 45 degree angle, as above. Stitch right sides together, trim turnings and press seam open.

Binding the edges

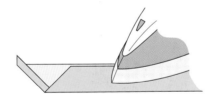

1 Cut the starting end of binding strip at a 45 degree angle, fold a 1/4in (6mm) turning to wrong side along cut edge and press in place. With wrong sides together, fold strip in half lengthways, keeping raw edges level, and press.

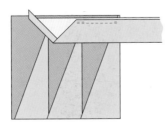

2 Starting at the centre of one of the long edges, place the doubled binding on to the right side of the quilt keeping raw edges level.

Stitch the binding in place starting 1/4in (6mm) in from the diagonal folded edge (see above). Reverse stitch to secure, and working 1/4in (6mm) in from edge of the quilt towards first corner of quilt. Stop 1/4in (6mm) in from corner and work a few reverse stitches.

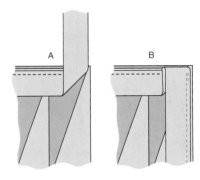

3 Fold the loose end of the binding up, making a 45 degree angle (see A). Keeping the diagonal fold in place, fold the binding back down, aligning the raw edges with the next side of the quilt. Starting at the point where the last stitch ended, stitch down the next side (see B).

4 Continue to stitch the binding in place around all the quilt edges in this way, tucking the finishing end

of the binding inside the diagonal starting section (see above).

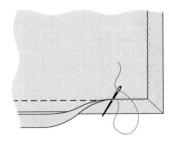

5 Turn the folded edge of the binding on to the back of the quilt. Hand stitch the folded edge in place just covering binding machine stitches, and folding a mitre at each corner.

Glossary of Terms

Appliqué The technique of stitching fabric shapes on to a background to create a design. It can be applied either by hand or machine with a decorative embroidery stitch, such as buttonhole, or satin stitch.

Backing The bottom layer of a quilt sandwich. It is made of fabric pieced to the size of the quilt top with the addition of about 3in (7.5cm) all around to allow for quilting take–up.

Basting or Tacking This is a means of holding two fabric layers or the layers of a quilt sandwich together temporarily with large hand stitches, or pins.

Batting or Wadding This is the middle layer, or padding in a quilt. It can be made of cotton, wool, silk or synthetic fibres.

Bias The diagonal grain of a fabric. This is the direction which has the most give or stretch, making it ideal for bindings, especially on curved edges.

Binding A narrow strip of fabric used to finish off the edges of quilts or projects; it can be cut on the straight grain of a fabric or on the bias.

Block A single design unit that when stitched together with other blocks create the quilt top. It is most often a square, hexagon, or rectangle, but it can be any shape. It can be pieced or plain.

Border A frame of fabric stitched to the outer edges of the quilt top. Borders can be narrow or wide, pieced or plain. As well as making the quilt larger, they unify the overall design and draw attention to the central area.

Chalk pencils Available in various colours, they are used for marking lines, or spots on fabric.

Cutting mat Designed for use with a rotary cutter, it is made from a special 'self–healing' material that keeps your cutting blade sharp. Cutting mats come in various sizes and are usually marked with a grid to help you line up the edges of fabric and cut out larger pieces.

Design Wall Used for laying out fabric patches before sewing. A large wall or folding board covered with flannel fabric or cotton batting in a neutral shade (dull beige or grey work well) will hold fabric in place so that an overall view can be taken of the placement.

Free–motion quilting Curved wavy quilting lines stitched in a random manner. Stitching diagrams are often given for you to follow as a loose guide.

Freezer Paper Paper which is plasticized on one side, usually sold on a roll. Originally used for wrapping meat for freezing it was found to adhere to fabric when pressed. It is useful for appliqué as it stays in place until peeled away without leaving any residue.

Fussy cutting This is when a template is placed on a particular motif, or stripe, to obtain interesting effects. This method is not as efficient as strip cutting, but yields very interesting results.

Grain The direction in which the threads run in a woven fabric. In a vertical direction it is called the lengthwise grain, which has very little stretch. The horizontal direction, or crosswise grain is slightly stretchy, but diagonally the fabric has a lot of stretch. This grain is called the bias. Wherever possible the grain of a fabric should run in the same direction on a quilt block and borders.

Grain Lines These are arrows printed on templates which should be aligned with the fabric grain.

Inset seams or setting–in A patchwork technique whereby one patch (or block) is stitched into a 'V' shape formed by the joining of two other patches (or blocks).

Patch A small shaped piece of fabric used in the making of a patchwork pattern.

Patchwork The technique of stitching small pieces of fabric (patches) together to create a larger piece of fabric, usually forming a design.

Pieced quilt A quilt composed of patches.

Quilting Traditionally done by hand with running stitches, but for speed modern quilts are often stitched by machine. The stitches are sewn through the top, wadding and backing to hold the three layers together. Quilting stitches are usually worked in some form of design, but they can be random.

Quilting hoop Consists of two wooden circular or oval rings with a screw adjuster on the outer ring. It stabilises the quilt layers, helping to create an even tension.

Rotary cutter A sharp circular blade attached to a handle for quick, accurate cutting. It is a device that can be used to cut up to six layers of fabric at one time. It must be used in conjunction with a 'self–healing' cutting mat and a thick plastic ruler.

Rotary ruler A thick, clear plastic ruler printed with lines that are exactly ?in (6mm) apart. Sometimes they also have diagonal lines printed on, indicating 45 and 60 degree angles. A rotary ruler is used as a guide when cutting out fabric pieces using a rotary cutter.

Sashing A piece or pieced sections of fabric interspaced between blocks.

Sashing Posts When blocks have sashing between them the corner squares are known as sashing posts.

Selvedges Also known as selvages, these are the firmly woven edges down each side of a fabric length. Selvedges should be trimmed off before cutting out your fabric, as they are more liable to shrink when the fabric is washed.

Stitch–in–the–ditch or Ditch quilting Also known as quilting–in–the–ditch. The quilting stitches are worked along the actual seam lines, to give a pieced quilt texture.

Template A pattern piece used as a guide for marking and cutting out fabric patches, or marking a quilting, or appliqué design. Usually made from plastic or strong card that can be reused many times. Templates for cutting fabric usually have marked grain lines which should be aligned with the fabric grain.

Threads One hundred percent cotton or cotton–covered polyester is best for hand and machine piecing. Choose a colour that matches your fabric. When sewing different colours and patterns together, choose a medium to light neutral colour, such as grey or ecru. Specialist quilting threads are available for hand and machine quilting.

Walking foot or Quilting foot This is a sewing machine foot with dual feed control. It is very helpful when quilting, as the fabric layers are fed evenly from the top and below, reducing the risk of slippage and puckering.

Biographies

Kim McLean

Kim began quilting in the early 1990's using Liberty prints in pastel shades. She attended a beginner's quilting class and within two years had acquired a huge fabric stash and won Best Of Show Quilts at the Sydney Quilt Show. She draws inspiration for her breathtaking applique quilts from her surroundings and travel within Australia and overseas. To find out more about Kim read A Quilter's Story on pages 52 - 55.

Pauline Smith

Pauline Smith has been a quilt maker and designer since a college visit to The American Museum in Bath in 1968. She makes most of Kaffe's quilts for the Rowan Patchwork And Quilting books, and as the Rowan patchwork co-ordinator, she works closely with everyone involved in producing the 'Patchwork and Quilting' series.

Sally Davis

Sally began quiltmaking in 1980 after experimenting with every known craft. It quickly became a love affair and passion. Sally owned a quilt shop called Quilt Connection where she met Liza and Kaffe and over 9 years encompassed her love of colour with their style and fabrics. Two of her quilts were featured in Rowan P&Q 4 and a Colourful Journey. After closing the store 2 years ago, Sally has been travelling around the country teaching and lecturing as well as working with Liza.

Roberta Horton

Roberta Horton of Berkeley, California has been a quiltmaker for over 30 years. She has taught and lectured worldwide. Her study and love of quilts has pushed her into developing many workshops and to the authoring of six books. Roberta was the recipient of the 2000 Silver Star Award presented by the International Quilt Association. This was in recognition of her lifetime body of work and the long-term effect it has had on quilting.

Brandon Mably

A regular contributor to the Rowan Patchwork books Brandon Mably has built a reputation as a quilt designer of simple, elegant quilts in restful colours. Brandon trained at The Kaffe Fassett Studio. He designs for the Rowan and Vogue Knitting magazine knitwear collections, and is the author of *Brilliant Knits* and *Knitting Color*. Brandon launched his first fabric designs for Rowan in 2008.

Mary Mashuta

California quiltmaker Mary Mashuta has been making quilts and wearables for over thirty years. She is a professionally trained teacher who has been teaching internationally since 1985. Her classes always stress easily understood colour and design. She knows that no quilter can own too much fabric, and she enjoys discovering new blocks to showcase personal collections. Mary has authored six books, the latest is *Foolproof Machine Quilting* and numerous magazine articles.

Pam Goecke Dinndorf

My relationship with colorful fabrics began as far back as I can remember—this fascination with color and pattern accompanied me through the fashion industry, interior design, and eventually designing quilt patterns under the name, Aardvark Quilts. Inspired by vintage quilts, repetitive shapes in daily life, and the plethora of glorious fabrics now available, I create quilts of simple design that allow the fabrics to shine. Kaffe's fabrics obviously provide me an endless source of joy and inspiration.

Liza Prior Lucy

Liza Prior Lucy first began making quilts in 1990. She was so enthralled by the craftspeople she met and by the generously stocked quilt fabric shops in the States that quiltmaking soon became a passion. Liza originally trained as a knitwear designer and produced features for needlework magazines. She also owned and operated her own needlepoint shop in Washington, D.C.
Liza met Kaffe when she was working as a sales representative for Rowan Yarns. They worked closely together to write and produce the quilts for the books *Glorious Patchwork*, *Passionate Patchwork* and *Kaffe Fassett's V&A Quilts*.

Experience Ratings

★ Easy, straightforward, suitable for a beginner.

★ ★ Suitable for the average pachworker and quilter.

★ ★ ★ For the more experienced patchworker and quilter.

Other ROWAN Titles Available

Seven Easy Pieces - Pauline Smith
The Impatient Patchworker - Jane Emerson
Patchwork And Quilting Book 4
A Colourful Journey
Kaffe Fassett's Quilt Road
Kaffe Fassett's Quilts In The Sun
Kaffe Fassett's Country Garden Quilts

Acknowledgements

We give a huge thank you to Robin Llywelyn, Corina Owen and all the staff at Portmeirion for their generosity and help when photographing this book, and for allowing us unrestricted access.

Portmeirion is owned by the Second Portmeirion Foundation, managed by Portmeirion Ltd., and is a registered charity. The village is open every day of the year from 09.30 - 17.30. For more information check out their website - www.portmeirion-village.com

All Drima and Sylko machine threads, Anchor embroidery threads, and Prym sewing aids, distributed in UK by Coats Crafts UK, P.O. Box 22, Lingfield House, Lingfield Point, McMullen Road, Darlington, Co. Durham, DL1 1YQ.
Consumer helpline: 01325 394237.

Anchor embroidery thread and Coats sewing threads, distributed in the USA by Coats & Clark,
3430 Toringdon Way, Charlotte, North Carolina 28277.
Tel: 704 329 5800.
Fax: 704 329 5027.

Prym products distributed in the USA by Prym-Dritz Corp,
950 Brisack Road, Spartanburg, SC 29303.
Tel: +1 864 576 5050. Fax: +1 864 587 3353,
e-mail: pdmar@teleplex.net

R O W A N

Green Lane Mill, Holmfirth, West Yorkshire, England
Tel: +44 (0) 1484 681881   Fax: +44 (0) 1484 687920   Internet: www.knitrowan.com
Email: mail@knitrowan.com

Printed Fabrics

When ordering printed fabrics please note the following codes which precede the fabric number and two digit colour code.

GP is the code for the Kaffe Fassett collection
PJ is the code for the Philip Jacobs collection
BM is the code for the Brandon Mably collection

The fabric collection can be viewed online at the following

www.westminsterfibers.com

QUILT INSTRUCTION CODES		THE AMERICAN CODES
Woven Multi Stripe		
Brown	WMSBR	WMULTI.BROWN
Fuchsia	WMSFU	WMULTI.FUCHS
Green	WMSGN	WMULTI.GREEN
Indigo	WMSIN	WMULTI.INDIG
Purple	WMSPU	WMULTI.PURPL
Teal	WMSTE	WMULTI.TEAL
Red	WMSRD	WMULTI.REDD
Ivory	WMSIV	WMULTI.IVORY
Woven Tone Stripe		
Citrus	WTSCN	W2TONE.CITRUS
Gold	WTSGD	W2TONE.GOLD
Red	WTSRD	W2TONE.REDD
Spice	WTSSI	W2TONE.SPICE
Suede	WTSSD	W2TONE.SUEDE
Green	WTSGN	W2TONE.GREEN
Woven Bold Stripe		
Fuchsia	WBSFU	WBDSTR.FUCHS
Gold	WBSGD	WBDSTR.GOLD
Lavender	WBSLV	WBDSTR.LAVEN
Teal	WBSTE	WBDSTR.TEAL
Woven Check		
Fuchsia	WCHFU	WCHECK.FUCHS
Mint	WCHMT	WCHECK.MINT
Pink	WCHPK	WCHECK.PINK

Distributors and Stockists

Overseas Distributors of Rowan Fabrics

AUSTRIA
Rhinetex
Geurdeland 7
6673 DR Andelst
The Netherlands
Tel: 31 488 480030
Email: info@rhinetex.com

AUSTRALIA
XLN Fabrics
2/21 Binney Road,
Kings Park
New South Wales 2148
Tel: 61-2 -9621-3066
Email: info@xln.co.zu

BELGIUM
Rhinetex
Geurdeland 7
6673 DR Andelst
The Netherlands
Tel: 31- 488- 480030
Email: info@rhinetex.com

BRAZIL
Coats Corrente Ltd
Rua Do Manifesto,
705 Ipiranga
Sao Paulo
SP 04209-00
5511-3247-8000

CANADA
Telio
625 Rue DesLauriers
Montreal, QC, Canada
Tel: 514- 271- 4607
Email: info@telio.com

DENMARK
Coats Expotex AB
Box 297
SE-401 24 Göteborg
Tel: -+46 31 72145-15
Fax: +46 31 471650

FINLAND
Coats Opti Crafts Oy
Ketjutie 3
04220 Kerava
Finland
Tel: 358-9-274871

FRANCE
Rhinetex
Geurdeland 7
6673 DR Andelst
The Netherlands
Tel: 31 488 480 0 30
Email: info@rhinetex.com

GERMANY
Rhinetex
Geurdeland 7
6673 DR Andelst
The Netherlands
Tel: 31 488 480030
Email: info@rhinetex.com

HUNGARY
Coats Crafts Hungary Kft.
H-7500 Nagyatád
Gyár utca 21.
www.coatscrafts.hu

ITALY
Coats Cucirini Srl
Viale Sarca 223
20126 Milano Mi
MILANO

JAPAN
Kiyohara & Co Ltd
4-5-2 Minamikyuhoji-Machi
Chuo-Ku
OSAKA
541-8506
Tel: 81 6 6251 7179

KOREA
Coats Korea Co Ltd,
5F Kuckdong B/D,
935-40 Bangbae-Dong,
Seocho-Gu, Seoul,
South Korea
Tel: 82- 2 -521- 6262

LITHUANIA
Coats Lietuva UAB
A.Juozapaviciaus g. 6/2,
LT-09310 Vilinius
Tel: 3705- 2730972
Fax: 3705 2723057
www.coatscrafts.lt

LUXEMBOURG
Rhinetex
Geurdeland 7
6673 DR Andelst
The Netherlands
Tel: 31 488 480 0 30
Email: info@rhinetex.com

NEW ZEALAND
Fabco Limited
280 School Road
P.O. Box 84-002
Westgate
AUCKLAND 1250
Tel: 64- 9- 411- 9996
Email: info@fabco.co.nz

NETHERLANDS
Rhinetex
Geurdeland 7
6673 DR Andelst
The Netherlands
Tel: 31 488 480 0 30
Email: info@rhinetex.com

NORWAY
Coats Expotex AB
Box 297
SE-401 24 Göteborg
Tel: +46 31 7214515
Fax: +46 31 471650

POLAND
Coats Polska Sp.z.o.o
ul. Kaczeńcowa 16
91-214 Lodz
Tel: 48 42 254 03 0400
www.coatscrafts.pl

PORTUGAL
Companhia de Linha Coats & Clark, SA
Quinta de Cravel
4430-968 Vila Nova de Gaia
Tel: 00 351- 223 770 700

SINGAPORE
Quilts and Calicos
163 Tanglin Road
03-13 Tanglin Mall
247933
Tel: 65- 688 74708

SOUTH AFRICA
Arthur Bales PTY Ltd
62 4th Avenue
PO Box 44644
Linden 2104
Tel: 27- 11- 888- 2401

SPAIN
Coats Fabra, S.A.
Sant Adriá, 20
E-08030 Barcelona
Tel: 00 +34 93- 290. 84. 00
Fax: +34 93-290.84.39

SWITZERLAND
Rhinetex
Geurdeland 7
6673 DR Andelst
The Netherlands
Tel: 31 488 480030
Email: info@rhinetex.com

SWEDEN
Coats Expotex AB
Box 297
SE-401 24 Göteborg
Tel: +46 31 7214515
Fax: +46 31 471650

TAIWAN
Long Teh Trading Co
3F N0 19-2 Kung Yuan Road
Taichung, Taiwan
Tel: 886-4-225-6698

UK
Rowan
Green Lane Mill
Holmfirth
HD9 2DX
United Kingdom
Tel: +44(0) 1484 681881
www.knitrowan.com
Email: mail@knitrowan.com

U.S.A
Westminster Fibers
3430 Toringdon Way
Suite 301,
Charlotte,
NC 28277
Tel: 704-329-5822
Email: fabric@westminsterfibers.com
www.westminsterfibers.com